Madagascar

WORLD BIBLIOGRAPHICAL SERIES

General Editors:
Robert G. Neville (Executive Editor)
John J. Horton

Robert A. Myers   Ian Wallace
Hans H. Wellisch   Ralph Lee Woodward, Jr.

John J. Horton is Deputy Librarian of the University of Bradford and currently Chairman of its Academic Board of Studies in Social Sciences. He has maintained a longstanding interest in the discipline of area studies and its associated bibliographical problems, with special reference to European Studies. In particular he has published in the field of Icelandic and of Yugoslav studies, including the two relevant volumes in the World Bibliographical Series.

Robert A. Myers is Associate Professor of Anthropology in the Division of Social Sciences and Director of Study Abroad Programs at Alfred University, Alfred, New York. He has studied post-colonial island nations of the Caribbean and has spent two years in Nigeria on a Fulbright Lectureship. His interests include international public health, historical anthropology and developing societies. In addition to *Amerindians of the Lesser Antilles: a bibliography* (1981), *A Resource Guide to Dominica, 1493-1986* (1987) and numerous articles, he has compiled the World Bibliographical Series volumes on *Dominica* (1987), *Nigeria* (1989) and *Ghana* (1991).

Ian Wallace is Professor of German at the University of Bath. A graduate of Oxford in French and German, he also studied in Tübingen, Heidelberg and Lausanne before taking teaching posts at universities in the USA, Scotland and England. He specializes in contemporary German affairs, especially literature and culture, on which he has published numerous articles and books. In 1979 he founded the journal *GDR Monitor*, which he continues to edit under its new title *German Monitor*.

Hans H. Wellisch is Professor emeritus at the College of Library and Information Services, University of Maryland. He was President of the American Society of Indexers and was a member of the International Federation for Documentation. He is the author of numerous articles and several books on indexing and abstracting, and has published *The Conversion of Scripts, Indexing and Abstracting: an International Bibliography* and *Indexing from A to Z*. He also contributes frequently to *Journal of the American Society for Information Science*, *The Indexer* and other professional journals.

Ralph Lee Woodward, Jr. is Director of Graduate Studies at Tulane University, New Orleans, where he has been Professor of History since 1970. He is the author of *Central America, a Nation Divided*, 2nd ed. (1985), as well as several monographs and more than sixty scholarly articles on modern Latin America. He has also compiled volumes in the World Bibliographical Series on *Belize* (1980), *Nicaragua* (1983), and *El Salvador* (1988). Dr. Woodward edited the Central American section of the *Research Guide to Central America and the Caribbean* (1985) and is currently editor of the Central American history section of the *Handbook of Latin American Studies*.

VOLUME 165

Madagascar

Hilary Bradt

Compiler

with

Mervyn Brown

CLIO PRESS

OXFORD, ENGLAND · SANTA BARBARA, CALIFORNIA
DENVER, COLORADO

British Library Cataloguing in Publication Data

Madagascar. – (World Bibliographical Series; vol. 165)
I. Bradt, Hilary.   II. Series
016.9691

ISBN 1–85109–179–3

Clio Press Ltd.,
55 St. Thomas' Street,
Oxford OX1 1JG, England.

ABC-CLIO,
130 Cremona Drive,
Santa Barbara,
CA 93116, USA.

Designed by Bernard Crossland.
Typeset by Columns Design and Production Services Ltd, Reading, England.
Printed and bound in Great Britain by
Bookcraft (Bath) Ltd., Midsomer Norton

THE WORLD BIBLIOGRAPHICAL SERIES

This series, which is principally designed for the English speaker, will eventually cover every country (and many of the world's principal regions), each in a separate volume comprising annotated entries on works dealing with its history, geography, economy and politics; and with its people, their culture, customs, religion and social organization. Attention will also be paid to current living conditions – housing, education, newspapers, clothing, etc.– that are all too often ignored in standard bibliographies; and to those particular aspects relevant to individual countries. Each volume seeks to achieve, by use of careful selectivity and critical assessment of the literature, an expression of the country and an appreciation of its nature and national aspirations, to guide the reader towards an understanding of its importance. The keynote of the series is to provide, in a uniform format, an interpretation of each country that will express its culture, its place in the world, and the qualities and background that make it unique. The views expressed in individual volumes, however, are not necessarily those of the publisher.

VOLUMES IN THE SERIES

Contents

Contents

Introduction

Madagascar, the world's fourth largest island which is about 1,000 miles long and 350 miles at its widest point, lies some 250 miles off the east coast of Africa, south of the equator. It is crossed by the Tropic of Capricorn near the southern town of Tuléar (Toliara). A chain of mountains runs down its length like a backbone bringing a sharp contrast in climates; broadly speaking the east is wet and the west is dry, with rainfall decreasing from north to south and desert conditions prevailing in the south-west. The north has its own microclimate influenced by the country's highest mountain (Maromokofro, 9,450 ft). The steep slopes of the eastern escarpment bear the remains of the dense rain forest which once covered all of the eastern section of the island. The western plain is wider and the climate drier, with forests of deciduous trees and acres of savanna grassland.

The most densely populated part of Madagascar is the old kingdom of Imerina, comprising the highlands around the capital Antananarivo. The city was called Tananarive by the French who ruled the country from 1895 to 1960, and imposed their own names on the most important towns. The country's rapidly-increasing population numbers over eleven million, with one-and-a-half million living in the capital. Other important towns are the main port of Tamatave (Toamasina) on the east coast, the northern port of Diego Suarez (Antsiranana) and the two southern ports, Tuléar (Toliara) and Fort Dauphin (Taolañaro).

When Madagascar broke away from Africa some 165 million years ago it probably carried with it the primitive ancestors of the mammals that are now found there, along with the reptiles which, at that time, dominated the earth. Others probably crossed the widening Mozambique channel on rafts of vegetation. The mammals which evolved on this mini-continent did not include large predators such as the big cats or pack-hunting dogs found in Africa, Asia or America. Nor did that major predator, man, appear on the scene until about 2,000 years ago. Animals had no need for long legs to escape their enemies, nor for large brains to outwit them. Evolution took a different course, with few families but great diversity within these groups including some thirty species of lower primates – the lemurs. All of Madagascar's indigenous mammals are unique to the island, and about 80 per cent of all living things there are found nowhere else in the world.

It is the wildlife that draws the modern visitor, tourist and scientist alike, but 2,000 years ago it was the restlessness of the people of Indonesia who arrived in their outrigger canoes to colonize the island. These colonists most likely took their time to reach Madagascar, sailing round the perimeter of the Indian Ocean and perhaps assimilating with tribes along the east coast of Africa before they made their landing on this new land. It is thought unlikely that they sailed directly across the 6,400 kilometres of ocean, although it has been proved possible by a modern Kon-Tiki style expedition. They brought their language (the Malagasy language belongs to the Malayo-Polynesian family), they brought their culture based on ancestor worship, and they brought their food staple: rice. Later they brought cattle, not just as food but as a source of wealth and for sacrifice to the ancestors. Rice and cattle have changed the face of the land. Forests have been cut and burned to make way for one or the other, and the unique flora and fauna is now under serious threat.

The first Europeans to sight Madagascar were the Portuguese in 1500, although there is evidence of earlier Arab settlements on the coast. There were unsuccessful attempts to establish French and British settlements during the next couple of centuries; these failed due to disease and hostile local people. By the early 1700s, the island had become a haven for pirates and slave-traders, and these were the Europeans who had the most influence on the Malagasy until a remarkable group of Welsh missionaries arrived in 1818 to spread the gospel under the auspices of the London Missionary Society (LMS).

Madagascar was at that time ruled by a worldly and pro-European king, Radama I, of the Merina tribe, who invited the LMS to send missionaries and artisans to teach crafts and light industry. The first to arrive in Tamatave were David Jones and Thomas Bevan, with their wives and children, but within a few weeks only Jones remained alive; the others had all died of fever. Jones retreated to Mauritius, but returned to Madagascar in 1820 to devote the rest of his life to its people, along with equally dedicated missionary teachers and artisans. The British influence was established and, apart from some ancient arabic texts, a written language was introduced for the first time using the roman alphabet.

Radama's widow and successor, Queen Ranavalona I, was determined to rid the land of Christianity and European influence, and reigned long enough largely to achieve her aim. However, the missionaries and European influence returned in greater strength after her death and in 1869 Christianity became the official religion of the Merina kingdom.

During this period of British influence, the French maintained a long-standing claim to Madagascar and in 1883 they attacked and occupied the main ports. The Franco-Malagasy War lasted thirty months, and was concluded by a harsh treaty giving France a form of protectorate over Madagascar. The Prime Minister, hoping for British support, managed to evade full acceptance of the protectorate but the British government signed away its interest in the Convention of Zanzibar in 1890. The French finally imposed their rule by invasion in 1895. For a year the country was a full protectorate and in 1896 Madagascar became a French colony. A year later Queen Ranalavona III was exiled to Algeria and the monarchy abolished.

Britain has played an important part in the military history of Madagascar. During the wars which preceded colonization British mercenaries trained the Malagasy army to fight the French. In 1942, when Madagascar was under the control of the Vichy French, the British invaded Madagascar to forestall the possibility of the Japanese Navy making use of the great harbour of Diego Suarez.

In 1943 Madagascar was handed back to France under a Free French Government. An uprising by the Malagasy against the French in 1947 was bloodily repressed and some 80,000 are said to have been killed. But the spirit of independence lived on and thirteen years later the country achieved full independence. The first president, Tsiranana, was pro-French, but in 1972 he stepped down in the face of increasing unrest and student demonstrations against French neo-colonialism. An interim government headed by General Ramanantsoa ended France's special position, and introduced a more nationalistic foreign and economic policy.

In 1975, after a period of turmoil, a Military Directorate handed power to a naval officer, Didier Ratsiraka, who had served as Foreign Minister under Ramanantsoa. Ratsiraka established the Second Republic, changing the country's name from the Malagasy Republic to The Democratic Republic of Madagascar. He introduced his own brand of 'Christian-Marxism' and his manifesto, set out in a 'little red book', was approved by referendum. Socialist policies such as the nationalization of banks followed. Within a few years the economy had collapsed and has remained in severe difficulties ever since. Ratsiraka was nevertheless twice re-elected, though there were claims of ballot rigging and intimidation.

Introduction

In 1991 a pro-democracy coalition called the Forces Vivres, in which the churches played an important part, organized a remarkable series of strikes and daily demonstrations calling for Ratsiraka's resignation. In August an estimated 500,000 demonstrators marched on the President's Palace. Though unarmed and orderly, they were fired on by the presidential guards and many died. Although Ratsiraka refused to resign, he was finally compelled to give up his executive powers and agree to a referendum which approved a new constitution and fresh elections. These took place in 1992/93 and were won by Albert Zafy, the Minister of Social Services under Ramanantsoa. The Third Republic, born in 1993, has embraced the principles of multi-party democracy and a free-market economy.

The Madagascar of today is one of the poorest countries in the world, a far cry from the optimistic predictions of some writers a hundred years ago; in 1895 a London economist wrote: 'Madagascar only requires the advent of railways and roads to make it one of the most prosperous commercial countries of the world', but with the Third Republic comes new hope. The late 1980s and early 1990s saw a surge of interest in the unique natural history and ethnology of the island, fuelled by some excellent television programmes. This has resulted in a ten-fold increase in tourism. The bureaucracy that hindered scientific expeditions in the past has now largely been lifted which will further add to the knowledge of the country. The present paucity of recent books about Madagascar should soon end.

Two languages have dominated literature on Madagascar: French and English. The few books published before the 19th century were divided about equally between the two, with Etienne de Flacourt, the French governor of the first settlement at Fort Dauphin making the most notable French contribution (1658), and Daniel Defoe being the best-known English writer. He wrote the best account of the pirates of Madagascar under the pseudonym Captain C. Johnson, and is credited with 'ghosting' the most popular book ever written about Madagascar, Robert Drury's Diary (1729). Drury was a young shipwrecked Englishman forced to serve the Sakalava and Mahafaly royal families as a slave.

The early 19th century brought the missionaries from the LMS and an explosion of books in English, good and bad, mostly purporting to be a history and social study of the island. James Sibree stands out as the most accomplished and prolific writer. His five books (and many other writings) on the island encompass 50 years; after his initial contract to oversee the building of the Martyr Memorial Churches he returned to England to be ordained as a minister, before coming back to Madagascar as a missionary teacher and principal of the LMS

College in Antananarivo. William Ellis, the other great British writer of the period, was the 'foreign secretary' of the LMS, and managed to visit Antananarivo during the latter days of Queen Ranavalona's oppressive rule. He returned after her death to supervise the return of the missionaries. Two of his books deal with these episodes, but he also wrote the first substantial history of the island.

The British involvement with the ruling Hova's struggle against the French in 1890 produced some notable books by, among others, the correspondents of *The Times* and *Telegraph* who witnessed the French military occupation. Once the island had become a colony the British influence declined and until independence there were few books written in English. An exception were those by participants or observers of the British invasion of Madagascar in 1942. The most important French writer in the years leading up to the French conquest and into the 20th century was the great explorer and naturalist, Alfred Grandidier. He contributed many volumes, latterly with the help of his son Guillaume who wrote under his own name after his father's death. The French Jesuits filled the gap left by the LMS for studies of the Malagasy people and their customs. Later French writers included Hubert Deschamps, who wrote the best history in the French language, and in modern times an increasing number of books by Malagasy authors – mostly writing in French – has been published.

It is only in the last two decades that books on Madagascar in English again became available to the general public, inspired mainly by the wildlife. Alison Jolly combined scientific research with a highly readable style to bring the fauna, particularly lemurs, to the general public, and the popular naturalist/authors David Attenborough and Gerald Durrell have both written enthusiastically about Madagascar. Recently the island has been a popular destination for travel writers, including Dervla Murphy who visited the island (somewhat painfully) in 1982.

My selection of titles in this bibliography reflects the importance of books in the French language and quite a large percentage have been included since they cover subjects or aspects about which there is nothing in English.

Items are listed in alphabetical order by author, under a series of sub-headings. Some books which were written originally as historical or cultural accounts (usually by members of the London Missionary Society) have been listed under 'Travellers' Accounts' since their value as accurate historical accounts is limited, whereas their first hand descriptions of the times make them both interesting and informative. The narratives with a strong religious bias have been entered under 'Religion'.

Introduction

Acknowledgements

My deep gratitude is owed to Sir Mervyn Brown, ex-British ambassador to Madagascar and Britain's greatest expert on the country's history, who gave me access to his large collection of books on Madagascar and provided an evaluation on their relative merits. In addition he checked and commented on all the entries he was familiar with. In terms of knowledge, this is partly his book. For the compilation and evaluation of titles in French I am indebted to my Malagasy assistant, Mrs Gisèle Alexander, whose work in the Bodleian Library in Oxford netted many additional English-language titles. Thanks are also due to Alan Hickling in Antananarivo for providing information on titles available only in Madagascar, to Gordon and Merlin Munday, and to Clare and Johan Hermans for help with the flora section. Caroline Harcourt gave valuable advice on fauna, Beverly Mendheim helped with literature, and David Freedman's extensive library had many unusual titles on language, philately and numismatics.

Much of my research was done at the School of Oriental and African Studies (SOAS) in London, who have inherited the world's largest private collection of books pertaining to Madagascar – the Hardyman Collection. James Hardyman, formerly a missionary in Madagascar, kindly donated his collection in 1991 when it became too large for him to house. At the time of going to press this collection is only partly catalogued; when finished it will be invaluable to those doing research on all aspects of Madagascar. My final thankyou goes to Mr Hardyman for his hospitality and introduction to the literature of Madagascar.

Hilary Bradt,
Farnham Common,
Buckinghamshire.
August 1993

The Country and its People

Accounts published in the pre-colonial period (1600-1895)

1 **Histoire physique, naturelle et politique de Madagascar.** (Physical, natural history and political history of Madagascar.)
Alfred Grandidier, Guillaume Grandidier. Paris: [various publishers], 1875-1900. 5 vols.
A monumental series consisting of several 'tomes' within five massive volumes. These represent the life work of Alfred Grandidier and his son Guillaume. Alfred first came to Madagascar in 1865, returned in 1866, and finally spent two years on the island (1868-69). Every aspect of Madagascar is covered in this encyclopaedic work: history; ethnography; geography and natural history – notably on the lemurs and birds. The Grandidier library is housed at Tsimbazaza, in Antananarivo.

2 **Madagascar and its people.**
James Sibree. London: The Religious Tract Society. 1870. 576p.
Sibree was an architect sent to Madagascar by the London Missionary Society to build the Martyr Memorial Churches following the anti-Christian reign of Queen Ranavalona. On his return to England he was ordained as a minister and came back to Madagascar to work as a teacher. He lived in Madagascar for 50 years. His introduction to the country is well written and carefully observed. There is an interesting appendix note on the recently-discovered egg of the aepyornis, or elephant bird. Sibree correctly identified it (others had guessed that it might be from a giant penguin or bird of prey). The book is illustrated with etchings.

3 Madagascar: the great African island.
James Sibree. London: Trubner. 1880. 372p. maps.
The author described his book as 'A popular account of recent researches in the physical geography, geology, and exploration of the country and its natural history and botany; and in the origin and divisions, customs and language, superstitions, folklore and religious beliefs and practices of the different tribes'. As always he achieves his aim with lucidity and warmth, mixing accurate scientific observation with his personal experiences. A few engravings provide illustrations.

Colonial period (1895-1960)

4 Madagascar.
Hubert Deschamps. Paris: Presses Universitaire de France, 1968. 122p. maps. (Que sais-je, no. 529).
Deschamp was a professor at the Sorbonne, who had served as a colonial officer in Madagascar and wrote various books about the country. This is a general introduction to the French colonial period between 1896 and 1960. Sections cover geography, the economy, politics and social aspects. The book is clearly laid out and easy to read, its strongest point being the detailed information on geography and the analysis of the economy. Some topics, such as the Malagasy culture and influence of the British are almost ignored, with the bias in favour of the colonial efforts to 'improve and civilize' Madagascar.

5 Madagascar.
D. Marcuse. In: *Peoples of all nations*. Edited by J. A. Hammerton. London: [n.p.], 1923. p. 3,383-427.
The 'Peoples of all nations' series of booklets, which eventually covered almost all the countries in the world, was aimed at young people and therefore contained heavy moral overtones. This issue, which may be viewed in the Hardyman Collection (SOAS), provides a good overview of all the Malagasy ethnic groups and is illustrated with excellent contemporary photographs.

6 Madagascar: land of the man-eating tree.
Chase S. Osborn. New York: Republic Publishing Company, 1924. 443p.
An overview of Madagascar written from the perspective of the 1920s by an American with enthusiasm and humour, if not total accuracy. He confesses that he never found a man-eating tree – the title is to attract the reader's interest. However, he does include a traveller's tale, written in 1878, describing in detail the triffid-like tree devouring a woman. Chapters cover history, ethnology, natural history, etc.; he is good on the contemporary way of life of the Malagasy people, and the book is well-illustrated with photographs.

Post-colonial (1960-)

7 Africa South of the Sahara.

London: Europa, 1972- . Annual. (Regional Surveys of the World).
This is the definitive survey and reference guide to the area, which includes Madagascar. Revised and updated annually, it cannot be bettered for recent information on Madagascar. The section comprises physical and social geography, recent history, and economy, each written by an expert in the field; followed by a statistical survey and directory.

8 A glance at Madagascar.

Antananarivo: Librairie tout pour l'école, 1973. 120p. maps.
This is an excellent little book, written by a British resident, giving an overview of the country. It is particularly useful on aspects that do not date, such as the description of the different ethnic groups, their customs and beliefs.

9 Civilisation de l'est et du sud-est: archeologie, anthropologie sociale et art de Madagascar. (Civilization of the east and south-east: archaeology, social anthropology and art of Madagascar.)

Musée d'Art et Archéologie. Tananarive: Université de Madagascar, 1974. 210p.
This is a series of papers presented by university researchers and lecturers, comprising fourteen essays in French and one in Malagasy. The subjects vary from the immigration of Arabs to Madagascar, to legends and archaeological surveys. A companion volume covers the south-west.

10 Provinces malgaches. (Malagasy provinces.)

Philippe Oberlé. Paris: Kintana, 1979. 228p.
The emphasis of this work is on history, and the volume is well illustrated with many black-and-white and colour photographs. Though now somewhat dated the book is of value to visitors who want in-depth information on places of tourist interest.

11 Tananarive et l'Imerina. (Tananarive and Imerina.)

Philippe Oberlé. Antananarivo: Librairie de Madagascar; Paris: Editions Presence Africaine, 1976. 184p.
This is a very useful and informative book despite its publication date. There are excellent descriptions of the capital and the villages in its vicinity, putting them into their historical context. Aimed at both residents and tourists, with many black-and-white photographs to show how the population centres have changed during this century, this book provides valuable details on a relatively small area of the highlands.

12 The great red island: a biography of Madagascar.

Arthur Stratton. London: Macmillan, 1965. 368p.
A racy, readable, and journalistic survey of Madagascar around the time of independence, this is an enjoyable book if the reader does not take it too seriously.

Pictorial books

13 **Madagascar.**
Hilary Bradt. Bourne End, England: Aston, 1988. 96p.
A collection of colour photographs showing all aspects of Madagascar: the people; the land; and the natural world. The work is aimed at the general reader and the photographs are accompanied by a text which provides an informative account of each of the topics considered.

14 **Madagascar, ma-terre-aux-mille-contrastes.** (Madagascar, my land of many contrasts.)
Jacques Hannebicque. Laval, France: Siloë, 1989. 176p.
This is a volume of high quality photographs of the different regions and people of Madagascar. Particularly interesting are the 'yesterday and today' photographs of well-known places.

15 **Madagascar, mon-île-au-bout-du-monde.** (Madagascar, my island at the end of the world.)
Jacques Hannebicque. Laval, France: Siloë, 1987. 192p.
The text and photographs in this large-format book show the author's affection for his birthplace. With an informative text and high-quality illustrations, he depicts the charm and contrasts of Madagascar.

16 **Madagascar: a world out of time.**
Photographs by Frans Lanting, essays by John Mack, Alison Jolly.
New York: Aperture, 1990. 144p.
A collection of one hundred spectacular colour photographs by one of the world's leading wildlife and travel photographers. Lanting has emphasized the contrasting aspects of beauty and environmental degradation which characterize Madagascar. The essays are written by two experts in their field: Dr Jolly in natural history and conservation, and Dr Mack in ethnology.

17 **Madagascar.**
Christian Vaisse. Paris: Arthaud, 1990. 192p.
A 'coffee table' book of high-quality photographs, mainly illustrating the landscape and Malagasy way of life. There is an interesting section of early photographs. The text is written in French.

The Malagasy Republic: Madagascar today.
See item no. 109.

Collection des oeuvrages anciens concernant Madagascar.
(A collection of ancient works concerning Madagascar.)
See item no. 111.

Madagascar, an historical and descriptive account of the island and its former dependencies.
See item no. 135.

Madagascar before the conquest: the island, the country, and the people.
See item no. 140.

Madagascar: politics, economics and society.
See item no. 225.

Madagascar.
See item no. 247.

Sainte-Marie de Madagascar: insularité et économie du girofle. (Sainte-Marie of Madagascar: insularity and economy of cloves.)
See item no. 256.

Geography

General

18 **Madagascar: étude géographique et économique.** (Madagascar: geographical and economic study.)
G. Bastian. Paris: Nathan, 1967. 192p. maps.
This is still the standard geography textbook in Madagascar. It is divided into four parts covering the natural environment, the human aspect, economics, and finally discusses five regions in detail. Illustrated by many maps, charts and photographs, this is an informative and helpful work.

19 **Madagascar, Mauritius, and other east-African islands.**
C. Keller. London: Swan Sonnenschein. 1901. 242p.
The geography section still has some usefulness, although the author has mainly drawn from the works of Grandidier.

20 **Le Lac Alaotra: étude preliminaire.** (Lake Alaotra: preliminary study.)
Tananarive: L'Institut Geographique National, 1962. 96p.
This exhaustive study, commissioned by the Ministry of Agriculture and in atlas format, covers every possible aspect of this lake in the north-east of Madagascar. It is illustrated with numerous maps and graphs. One can only guess at the purpose of the study in the knowledge that in the early 1990s this is one of the most environmentally disastrous areas in Madagascar.

21 **Biogeography and ecology in Madagascar.**
Edited by G. Richard-Vindard, R. Battistini. The Hague, Holland: Junk. 1972. 265p.
Included in this wide-ranging work are geography and geology, climatology, flora, description of forest types, erosion and soil degradation, rivers and streams, man and the environment, subfossils, coral reefs, insects and arachnids. There are chapters in

6

French on soils, molluscs and reptiles, carnivores and lemurs. Also included are human diseases and their relation to the environment, and the problems of nature conservation. The comprehensive coverage and detailed information make this an outstanding reference book.

Geology

22 **Description géologique du massif ancien de Madagascar.**
(Geological description of the ancient massif of Madagascar.)
Henri Besairie. Tananarive: Service Géologique, 1968-1971. 6 vols.

The main geological features of Madagascar are a Precambrian crystalline basement forming the eastern two-thirds of the island, overlaid with laterite; a region in the south and west of Jurassic, Cretaceous and Tertiary sedimentary rocks; and volcanic outcrops. This series, published by the Ministry of Industry and Mines, surveys the entire country in great detail. The volumes are: no. 1, *Centre nord et centre nord-est* (central north and central north-east) (1968); no. 2 *La région orientale entre le Mangoro et Vangaindrano* (The eastern region between the Mangoro and Vangaindrano) (1969); no. 3 *Le région centrale (i). Le système du graphite, groupe d'Ambatolampy*. (The central region (i). The graphite system of the Ambatolampy group) (1969); no. 4 *Le région centrale (ii). Le système du Vohibory: serie schisto-quartzo-calcaire, groupe d'Amborompotsy* (The Vohibory system: schist-quartzite-limestone series, Amborompotsy group) (1969); no. 5 *Le sud* (The south) (1970); and no. 6 *L'extrème nord* (The extreme north) (1971). By the same author and publisher is *Géologie de Madagascar* (Geology of Madagascar) (1971). The classic work on the minerals of Madagascar is *Minéralogie de Madagascar* (Mineralogy of Madagascar) by Alfred Lacroix (Paris: Challamel, 1922-3. 3 vols).

23 **Mineral resources of the Malagasy Republic.**
Thomas G. Murdock. Washington, DC: United States Department of the Interior, 1963. 147p. bibliog.

This book discusses the importance of the mineral wealth of Madagascar and its outlook according to the needs of the United States of America. The study includes a survey of the geography and population of Madagascar, as well as the mineral riches, the economy, and political and legal factors affecting the mineral development of the country. The book includes an analysis of the relationship between Madagascar and the United States, and a list of available minerals, fuel and energy.

Cartography

24 **Atlas de Madagascar.** (Atlas of Madagascar.)
    Tananarive: Institut Geographique National, 1971.
Excellent coloured maps show physical geography, human geography, rural geography, resources and industry, communications, various amenities (sanitation, hotels, missions) and regional divisions.

25 **Central and southern Africa/Madagascar.**
    Harrow, England: Michelin, revised annually. (Main Road Series, no. 955).
This is the most frequently updated map of Madagascar, although its small scale of 1:4,000,000 limits its use.

26 **La cartographie de Madagascar.** (The cartography of Madagascar.)
    Gabriel Gravier.   Rouen, France: Cacniard, 1896. 470p. maps.
This is an important work which describes, and where possible reproduces as foldout illustrations, every map of Madagascar from the earliest recognizable example published in 1492 to an accurate colour map from 1895. This work is also very useful for its accounts of all the expeditions and voyages of discovery to Madagascar, with mention of the cartographers.

27 **Madagascar.**
    Budapest: Kartografiai, 1991.
This map, which is at the scale of 1:2,000,000, has been issued under different covers by several publishers. It is reasonably accurate with a useful index of place names on the back.

28 **Madagasikara.** (Madagascar.)
    Antananarivo: Foiben-Taosarintanin'i Madagasikara, 1992.
This is the most readily-available map of the country and is at a scale of 1:2,00,000. It is updated fairly regularly. It has a city map of Antananarivo on the reverse, and an index. Foiben-Taosarintanin'i Madagasikara (the government mapping agency) has also published maps of eleven regions at a scale of 1:500,000; and two islands of tourist interest, Nosy Be and Sainte Marie, at a scale of 1:80,000 and 1:100,000 respectively.

Histoire physique, naturelle et politique de Madagascar. (Physical, natural history and political history of Madagascar.)
See item no. 1.

Carte internationale du tapis végétal et conditions écologique. Notice de la carte Madagascar. (International map of vegetation cover and ecological conditions. Notes on the Madagascar map.)
See item no. 74.

Madagascar, an historical and descriptive account of the island and its former dependencies.
See item no. 135.

Travellers' Accounts

Pre-19th century

29 **A narrative of the loss of the Winterton East Indiaman.**
George Buchan.   Edinburgh: Waugh & Innes; London: J. Hatchard &
Son, L. B. Sealey, T. Hamilton, 1820. 256p.

The full title is 'A narrative of the loss of the Winterton East Indiaman, wrecked on the coast of Madagascar in 1792 and the sufferings connected with that event, to which is subjoined a short account of the natives of Madagascar, with suggestions as to their civilisation by a passenger on the ship'. There were 280 people on board this ship which went aground near Tulear. Most survived to reach the town where they were welcomed with great hospitality by King Baba. The sufferings were during their ten-month wait at King Baba's court while one of the crew went by yawl to Mozambique to look for a ship large enough to rescue them. This book is valuable as a reference to the way of life in south-west Madagascar at that time.

30 **Madagascar; or Robert Drury's journal during fifteen years' captivity on that island.**
Robert Drury.   London: W. Meadows, 1729. 350p.

Reprinted six times before 1890, this is probably the most popular book ever published on Madagascar. Drury was shipwrecked on the south coast and kept as a slave for fifteen years. Some have doubted its authenticity, but those with knowledge of the area generally believe the story to be true, although some passages are very similar to Flacourt, and Defoe may have contributed to it. Whether or not some parts were 'ghosted' it is a fascinating and exciting story which deserves its popularity.

31 **Histoire de la grande isle de Madagascar.** (History of the great island of
Madagascar.)
Etienne de Flacourt. Paris: de Luyne. 1658. 384p. map.

Flacourt was sent to Madagascar in 1648 by the Compagnie des Indes Orientales (East
Indian Company) to regain control over the French colony at Fort Dauphin. He was
largely unsuccessful but provided the earliest firsthand account of the island. The first
part of the book is a description of the island, and of the people and flora and fauna of
the south-east. The illustrations of what he claims to have seen are delightful, they
include rhinoceros and penguins, as well as reasonably accurate pictures of lemurs and
other native animals and plants. The second part is a detailed account of the French
colony during the years 1642-55.

32 **A paradox prooving that the inhabitants of Madagascar, or St Laurence,
(in temporall things) are the happiest people in the world; whereunto is
prefixed, a briefe and true description of that island, the nature of the
climate and conditions of the inhabitants, and their special affection to the
English above all other nations. With most probable arguments of a
hopeful and fit plantation of a colony there, in respect of the fruitfulness
of the soyle, the benignity of the ayre, and the relieving of our English
ships, both to and from the East Indies.**
Walter Hamond. London: Nathaniell Butter, 1640. 37p.

This is a charming little book written by a passionate advocate of British colonization
in Madagascar who spent four months on what was then 'the greatest known island in
the world'. His observations on the Malagasy have been borne out by subsequent
research and, unusually for the times, his natural history is accurate: he notes that
'beasts of prey, as lions, tigers, woolves, and the like we saw none'. The second part of
the book, elaborating on the 'paradox' of the happy Malagasy, takes the form of an
empassioned plea to the powers that be to consider the state of grace of these people,
being naked (as Adam), and lacking in the products of civilization such as alcohol,
jewels, arms, rich food. . . He concludes by asking 'the mercies of God towards this
people, whose simplicity hath herein made them more happy than our too dear bought
knowledge hath advantaged us'.

33 **The voyages made by Sieur D.B. to the islands Dauphine or Madagascar
and Bourbon or Mascarene in the years 1669, 70, 71, and 72.**
Translated and edited by Captain Pasfield Oliver. London: David
Nutt, 1897. 160p. maps. bibliog.

Sieur De Bois was a member of an expedition dispatched by King Louis XIV with
letters of reprimand to the Marquis de Montdevergue who had failed to establish an
effective colony in the Fort Dauphin area. The author was incapacitated by malaria
during most of his stay in Madagascar, but there are some interesting accounts of the
country in the 17th century, with some probably accurate details on the customs of the
people. He notes that the Malagasy formerly treated whites like gods, but have
changed their attitude 'by the bad examples which the Europeans have had, who glory
in the sin of luxury in this country. . .'. The book is illustrated with some interesting
engravings and early photographs from the late 19th century.

34   **A voyage to Madagascar and the East Indies.**
The Abbé Rochon.   London: [n.p.], 1792. 475p. map.
The author describes himself as a 'Member of Academics of Sciences of Paris and
Petersburgh, Astronomer of the marine, keeper of the King's philosophical cabinet,
inspector of machines, money, etc.' The Madagascar section is basically a history of
the island as then known, and the author is highly critical of Flacourt and his
administration. In 1768 he witnessed the collapse, due to disease, of the French
establishment at Foulepoint on the east coast, and makes some interesting comments
on the adverse effects on the climate of the practice of deforestation, which was
already prevalent.

The 19th century

35   **Among the Malagasy: an unconventional record of missionary experience.**
John A. Houlder.   London: James Clarke, 1912. 320p.
The author arrived in Madagascar in 1871 and left in 1896 because of the war with
France. He travelled quite widely in the course of his missionary activities and
although this is a rather dull book he does provide some interesting insights into the
country under the control of prime minister Rainilaiarivony. The book is well-
illustrated with photographs and black-and-white paintings of some of the incidents
described.

36   **Through western Madagascar in quest of the golden bean.**
Walter A. Marcuse.   London: Hurst & Blackett, 1914. 322p. map.
The author correctly points out that little has been written about western Madagascar.
The 'golden bean' is the Madagascar butter-bean, which was introduced by American
whalers in 1864 and did well in the absence of its natural pests. The British started
plantations of this bean, and the author studied how the limited commercial success of
the venture affected the Sakalava people of the region. He also studied the industries
of cattle-raising and rubber. One chapter is entitled 'Ways of communication and
commerce'. This is an enjoyable travelogue which is full of good information and well
illustrated with a large number of photographs.

37   **Twelve months in Madagascar.**
Joseph Mullens.   London: James Nisbet, 1875. 334p.
The author was sent out to Madagascar by the London Missionary Society shortly after
Christianity was adopted as the official religion by Radama II. This king succeeded
Queen Ranavalona I who had expelled the missionaries from Madagascar during her
xenophobic reign. Mullens travelled in Betsileo, Imerina, Majunga, Lake Itasy, and
'saw the religious life of the people on the large scale'. The book provides a good eye-
witness account of that period, and there is a particularly interesting chapter entitled
'How it strikes a stranger'.

38   **The last travels of Ida Pfeiffer.**
      Ida Pfeiffer, translated by H. W. Dulcken.   London: Routledge, Warne
      & Routledge, 1861. 338p.

Ida Pfeiffer was a remarkable Austrian woman, born in 1797, who twice travelled
round the world, the first time in 1848. Before her second journey Alexander von
Humboldt tried to dissuade her from visiting Madagascar. He was evidently right. She
became embroiled in a plot against Queen Ranavalona and witnessed the torture and
martyrdom of the Christians and the last days of Jean Laborde (a remarkable
Frenchman who introduced light industry to Madagascar) before his expulsion. After
escaping with her life, the hardships suffered during the journey to the coast led to her
death a year later. She writes in journal form, from a position of cultural superiority.
Though some of her attitudes may jar the modern reader, this is a fascinating account
of a dangerous and colourful period of Madagascar's history.

39   **From Fianarantsoa to Ikongo.**
      George A. Shaw.   Tananarive: Friends Foreign Mission Association,
      1875. 21p.

This work is interesting in that it covers the central-south part of the country, whereas
most contemporary accounts by missionaries describe Imerina and the east coast ports.
There is a good description of the Sakalava, but the ethnological observations are
strongly biased towards a Christian standpoint. The book contains a vocabulary in
Hova, Sakalava and English.

Colonial period (1895-1960)

40   **Voyage à Madagascar 1889-1890.** (Voyage to Madagascar 1889-1890.)
      Dr Louis Catat.   Paris: Administration de l'Univers Illustré, 1894.
      410p. map.

The author travelled throughout Madagascar shortly after the French colonized the
island and during the last years of the monarchy. The book is different from other
contemporary accounts, being written by a doctor rather than a missionary. This is a
large book – the 19th century equivalent of a coffee table book – and is full of beautiful
etchings which gives it interest even to non-French-speaking readers.

41   **Across Madagascar.**
      Olive Murray Chapman.   London; Melbourne: Ed. J. Burrow, 1942.
      144p. map.

The author travelled alone in 1939 through Madagascar, mostly by car but also by
filanzana (litter). Her interest was in the remote tribes of the area and she covered
2,000 to 3,000 miles, from Majunga to Tananarive, and to Tuléar and Fort Dauphin.
She gives good descriptions of the customs of various ethnic groups, particularly those
of the south, and is more objective than most missionary accounts. However, the
natural history is inaccurate and the writing style pedestrian.

13

42   **The Madagascar I love.**
Arkady Fiedler.   London: Orbis, 1946. 187p.
An enjoyable book by a Polish national who lived in a small village in north-east Madagascar during a period when few foreigners were recording their impressions. He writes with affection and humour, describing incidents which well illustrate the Malagasy way of life at that time.

43   **Trader Horn in Madagascar: the waters of Africa.**
Alfred Aloysius Horn, edited by Ethelreda Lewis.   London: Cape, 1932. 256p.
This book, written under a pseudonym, is a reprint of a work first published in 1929 as *The life and works of Alfred Aloysius Horn III, the waters of Africa*. The hero was a famous explorer in Africa whose adventures captured popular imagination in Holywood films. This is in the 'rattling good yarn' category, and much of the Madagascar section is fictitious.

44   **Beyond the utmost purple rim: Abyssinia, Somaliland, Kenya Colony, Zanzibar, Comoros, Madagascar.**
Edward Alexander Powell.   London: John Long, 1925. 431p. maps.
The Madagascar section is on p. 347-418. This is a personal narrative by an American of an underdocumented period. Details that stand out are the descriptions of transport: a 'mono-pousse' which is a 'chair slung over a bicycle wheel', and the 'boeuf-cheval' (with accompanying photograph) which is an ox (zebu) broken to the saddle. There is also a description of the train journey from Tamatave to Antananarivo.

Post-colonial (1960-)

45   **Distant shores.**
Sally Crook.   London: Impact, 1990. 200p. map.
This is the account of a voyage by traditional canoe from Bali to Madagascar, proving that such a journey would have been possible for the early settlers of Madagascar who are known to have originated in Indonesia. The *Sarimanok*, a 60 ft double outrigger canoe, was constructed entirely from materials in use 2,500 years ago. The story of this remarkable journey is told by the only woman on board, a nutritionist who struggled to provide balanced meals using ingredients and cooking methods appropriate to the period.

46   **Dancing with the dead: a journey through Zanzibar and Madagascar.**
Helena Drysdale.   London: Hamish Hamilton, 1991. 273 pages. map.
The journey was inspired by the author's discovery of an ancestor who traded in the south-west Indian Ocean in the early 19th century and who corresponded with Queen Ranavalona. About two-thirds of the book concerns Madagascar, where she travelled extensively and adventurously. The book's title comes from the celebration of *famadihana*, or 'bone-turning' which she witnessed, highlighting the relationship between her interest in her own ancestor and the Malagasy veneration of theirs.

Entertaining and well-written, this is currently the most accurate portrayal of Madagascar from the point of view of an independent traveller.

47 Muddling through in Madagascar.
Dervla Murphy.   London: John Murray, 1985. 274p. map.

Dervla Murphy is a travel writer of distinction. With her teenage daughter she journeyed on foot through the mountains of Ankaratra, near Antananarivo but seldom visited by foreigners, and by a variety of vehicles down the bone-shaking Route Nationale 7 to the south. The author puts their travels in the context of Madagascar's complicated historical and social framework and paints a vivid picture of the Malagasy they meet. The book brims with humour although the reader is left agreeing with the reviewer who commented: 'Dervla Murphy's appetite for discomfort verges on the Gothic'.

48 The last of the dog-headed men.
Alex Shoumatoff.   In: *African madness*. New York: Knopf, 1988.
p. 45-89.

This is one of a series of essays about travel in Africa. The author is an established travel writer, and although his few weeks in Madagascar were by no means adventurous, he is an accurate observer and puts Madagascar in the context of its environmental problems; the 'dog-headed men' are the indri, one of the island's endangered lemurs. As a short introduction to Madagascar this chapter serves its purpose well.

Zoo quest to Madagascar.
See item no. 53.

The aye-aye and I.
See item no. 55.

Lemurs of the lost world.
See item no. 58.

An ancient account of Madagascar.
See item no. 113.

Madagascar revisited.
See item no. 131.

Three visits to Madagascar during the years 1853-1854-1856.
See item no. 132.

Madagascar and the Malagasy.
See item no. 134.

Travel Guides

49   **Sur les routes de Madagascar.** (On the roads of Madagascar.)
     J. P. Barboni.   Antananarivo: Societé Shell de Madagascar et de la
     Réunion, 1961. 102p.

A useful Shell Guide, published shortly after independence, and giving details of all
the major towns in Madagascar including their altitude, population, hotels, distance
from the nearest town, and possible excursions. Of historical and practical interest.

50   **Guide to Madagascar.**
     Hilary Bradt.   Chalfont St Peter, England: Bradt, 3rd ed. 1992. 246p.
     maps. bibliog.

An in-depth guide for travellers, frequently updated, illustrated in colour, and
including detailed background information on history, people, and natural history.

51   **The complete guide to the southwest Indian Ocean.**
     Iain Walker.   Port Argelès, France: Cornelius Books, 1993. 608p.
     maps.

The Madagascar section (p.137-318) is well-researched and covers a large number of
places, with plenty of hard information but it is a little short on background material
and is poorly organized.

52   **Madagascar and Comoros: a travel survival kit.**
     Robert Willcox.   Hawthorn, Australia: Lonely Planet Publications,
     1989. 190p. maps.

This is in the traditional Lonely Planet style of hard information on lodgings and
transport, with good maps and many colour illustrations. The Madagascar section
covers 132 pages.

Flora and Fauna

Travel and natural history

53 Zoo quest to Madagascar.
David Attenborough.   London: Lutterworth, 1961. 160p.
One of several natural history-cum-travel books linked with a 1960s television series.
David Attenborough was the first Englishman to bring the extraordinary Malagasy
wildlife to popular attention through the medium of television. Attenborough travelled
and filmed in the highlands and south of Madagascar, with a visit to Périnet in the east.
He describes accurately and entertainingly all the most interesting animals, particularly
the lemurs, in the context of his team's travels through the island and the people they
met. A highly readable, entertaining, and informative book.

54 Searching for the forest coconut in Madagascar.
John Dransfield.   In: *Plant hunting for Kew*. Edited by F. Nigel
Hepper.   London: HMSO [n.d.]. map.
The author was given the fruit of an unknown variety of palm and set out to identify it.
Two years later his search took him to the Bay of Antongil in north-west Madagascar
and through difficult terrain before the palm, now known as *Voanioala geradii*, was
found. This book clearly illustrates the challenges facing plant collectors in
Madagascar.

55 The aye-aye and I.
Gerald Durrell.   London: HarperCollins, 1992. 175p.
The aye-aye, Madagascar's most extraordinary lemur, is the focal point of this account
of collecting endangered species for captive breeding in the Jersey Wildlife
Preservation Trust. Other animals brought back to Jersey were gentle lemurs from the
Lake Alaotra region, and giant jumping rats from Morondava. The book is written
with the inimitable Durrell humour, providing an effortless way of absorbing
knowledge of Madagascar's natural history. Edward Whitley joined the expedition,
and describes it in 'The Durrells in Madagascar', p. 109-58 in *Gerald Durrell's army*

(London: John Murray, 1992). Whitley visited trainees of the Jersey Training Centre in their conservation areas throughout the world.

56 **Madagascar: a natural history.**
Ken Preston-Mafham. Oxford, New York: Facts on File (in association with Survival Anglia), 1991. 224p. maps. bibliog.

Illustrated with excellent colour photographs, this coffee table book is the most informative and enjoyable general work on the subject. Chapters cover the physical background, flora, invertebrates, amphibians and reptiles, birds, mammals other than lemurs, and lemurs. There is also a chapter on the national parks and reserves. The photographs identify many animals and plants that would otherwise remain a mystery to the interested amateur and the writing style is lively and easy to read.

57 **A naturalist in Madagascar.**
James Sibree. London: Seeley, Service & Co, 1915. 320p. maps.

The book is subtitled 'A record of observation, experiences and impressions made during a period of over fifty years' intimate association with the natives and study of the animal and vegetable life of the island'. This is more of a travelogue than a dry account of the natural history. Sibree is always immensely readable, with an observant eye for details of natural history and native customs.

58 **Lemurs of the lost world.**
Jane Wilson. London: Impact, 1990. 216p. map. bibliog.

In the north-west of Madagascar is the reserve of Ankarana, composed of eroded limestone cliffs, deep caves and almost inaccessible pockets of forest. The Crocodile Caves Expedition set out to explore this little-known area and to study rare species of lemur and other fauna, focusing on the sixty miles of caves which were said to be inhabited by crocodiles. This is an absorbing and well-written book which combines meticulous natural history observation with the joys and frustrations of travel in Madagascar. A scientific report on the expedition compiled by R. Walters, *The crocodile caves of Ankarana, 1986: an expedition to study and explore the limestone massif of Ankarana in northern Madagascar* (Bristol, England: Bristol City Museum, 1986. 90p.) is also available.

Environment and conservation

59 **Conservation aspects of the herpetofauna of Malagasy rain forests.**
Franco Andreone. Novara, Italy: Zoological Society La Torbiera, 1991. 46p. bibliog. (Scientific Report no. 1).

Written in Italian and English, this is a survey of the amphibians and reptiles in four rain forest zones: Perinet, Nosy Mangabe, Nahampoana and Montagne d'Ambre. It is mainly a list of the species found in those zones, although some behavioural observations are also made. For the specialist this is a useful little book, its value being enhanced by a good bibliography.

60 **Madagascar: an environmental profile.**
Edited by M. D. Jenkins. Cambridge, England; Gland, Switzerland: International Union for Conservation of Nature and Natural Resources, 1987. 374p. 3 maps.

A scientific and detailed overview of the ecology of Madagascar, including environmental pressures on protected areas and fauna recorded there, faunal species lists, and detailed accounts of some endangered species. Specific flora references are limited to a species list of succulents and palms and a section on ethnobotany (medicinal plants), the latter with a useful bibliography of database references.

61 **Madagascar.**
Edited by Alison Jolly, Philippe Oberlé, Roland Albignac. Oxford; New York; Toronto: Pergamon Press, 1984. 240p. 4 maps. bibliogs. (Key Environments).

Six chapters in this book are translated from *Madagascar: un sanctuaire de la nature* (q.v.) but there are five new ones on amphibians, chameleons, lemurs, carnivores, and insectivores. It is illustrated with numerous black-and-white photographs and line drawings. In comparison with the French edition, it is stronger on mammals and particularly lemurs, but the lack of colour photographs is a disadvantage. It remains one of the best English language non-scientific overviews of the natural history and is written in an accessible and lively style.

62 **A world like our own: man and nature in Madagascar.**
Alison Jolly. New Haven, Connecticut; London: Yale University Press, 1980. 272p. bibliog.

A highly readable, anecdotal and compassionate account of the natural history and ecology of Madagascar, and the pressures the impoverished rural population put on the endangered flora and fauna. Dr Jolly is the acknowledged expert in this field and though a little dated this is still the best book on the subject. This is a large-format coffee table book with numerous black-and-white and four pages of colour photographs.

63 **Planegap: an integrated planning model for ecotourism product development in Madagascar.**
James MacGregor. Antananarivo: Association Nationale pour la Gestion des Aires Protegées; Alexandria, USA: The Ecotourism Society, 1993. 16p.

This is a report on the National Ecotourism Seminar held in Madagascar in 1993. Ecotourism, or tourism that emphasizes nature and minimal impact on the environment, was agreed by the participants to be a means of financing conservation and raising awareness of threatened species and their habitats. The report outlines the steps necessary to develop ecotourism.

64 **Madagascar: revue de la conservation et des aires protégées.**
(Madagascar: revue of its conservation and the protected areas.)
Martin Nicoll, Olivier Langrand.   Gland, Switzerland: World Wide
Fund For Nature, 1989. 374p. 18 maps. bibliog.

This book provides a very detailed analysis of the work done by the World Wide Fund
For Nature (WWF) in surveying the national parks, reserves, and sites of biological
interest in Madagascar. The statistics for each protected area are set down with a note
on conservation measures and recommendations for the future. In the well-studied
reserves a list of vertebrates is included. A review of current conservation measures
and legislation with proposals for future priorities concludes this excellent book. The
very clear maps of the protected areas and environs are particularly valuable.

65 **Madagascar: un sanctuaire de la nature.** (Madagascar, a sanctuary of
nature.)
Edited by Philippe Oberlé.   Riedisheim, France: Kintana;
Antananarivo: Librairie de Madagascar, 1981. 117p. map. bibliog.

Considers the natural history of Madagascar as it was in 1981. In light of the scientific
research and discoveries made since that time this is inevitably dated, but it still
provides a useful and balanced description of flora and fauna written by French and
Malagasy experts on each subject, with 103 illustrations in colour. The chapter on the
naturalists of Madagascar, from Flacourt in the 17th century to modern times, is
particularly interesting. There are also chapters on marine life and freshwater fish.

66 **Manongarivo Special Reserve, Madagascar.**
Edited by N. Quansah.   London: Madagascar Environmental Research
Group, 1988. 170p.

This group is part of the Conservation Foundation at the Royal Geographical Society.
The reserve they surveyed is in the dry north-west of Madagascar. The expedition
noted the fauna, the level of protection, and made recommendations for future
protection. Members of the group also studied a rain forest reserve in the north-east: *A
survey of Ambatovaky Special Reserve, Madagascar,* edited by P. M. Thompson and
M. I. Evans. (London: M.E.R.G., 1991.).

67 **L'equilibre des ecosystèmes forestiers à Madagascar: actes d'un séminaire
international.** (The equilibrium of the forest ecosystems in Madagascar:
proceedings of an international seminar.)
Lala Rakotovao, Veronique Barre, Jeffrey Sayer.   Gland, Switzerland:
International Union for the Conservation of Nature, 1988. 338p.

The seminar covered a variety of conservation issues: the value of research; animal and
plant diversity and evolution; and forest management.

68 **A wildlife survey of Marojejy Nature Reserve.**
Edited by R. Safford, W. Duckworth.   Cambridge, England:
International Council of Bird Preservation, 1990. 183p. (Study Report
no. 40).

A report on an eight-week expedition to one of Madagascar's most important eastern
reserves. It contains an inventory of birds and mammals sighted, and some of the

reptiles and butterflies. The researchers also gathered ecological data relevant to conservation, reported on the degree of deforestation in and around the reserve, assessed the threats to the reserve and recommended future management and research.

Flora: general

69 **The flora of Madagascar.**
R. Baron. *Journal of the Linnean Society*, vol. 25 (1889-90), p. 246-94.
A general work on the plants of Madagascar. The different climatic regions and their plants are listed and described fairly superficially.

70 **Végétaux et groupements végétaux de Madagascar et des Mascareignes.**
(Vegetation and vegetation groups of Madagascar and the Mascarenes.)
Yvon Cabanis, Lucette Chabouis, Francis Chabouis.   Tananarive:
Bureau pour le developpement de la Production Agricole Agency de Madagascar, 1969-1970. 4 vols.
The flora of Madagascar is extraordinarily varied because of the striking difference in rainfall between the dry south and west of the island and the very wet eastern region. This is a work is aimed at the general public, and is well-illustrated with line drawings.

71 **Madagascar.**
Laurence Dorr, Lisa Barnett, Armand Rakotozafy.   In: *Floristic inventory of tropical countries: the status of plant systematics, collections, and vegetation, plus recommendations for the future.* Edited by David G. Campbell, David Hammond.   New York: New York Botanical Garden, 1989. p. 236-50. map. bibliog.
This review includes a description of the topography, climate and vegetation of the island, and lists major locations of herbarium specimens. Particularly useful is a section on 'Publications on the flora' and there is a good bibliography. A valuable overview.

72 **The highland flora of Madagascar.**
Blaise Du Puy.   *Quarterly Bulletin of the Alpine Garden Society*, vol. 59, no. 2 (June 1991), p. 134-48. map.
A detailed description of the plants growing above 1,500 m. The article is well-illustrated with photographs and contains recommended areas for finding highland flora.

73 **An introduction to the cultivated angraecoid orchids of Madagascar.**
Fred E. Hillerman, Arthur W. Holst.   Portland, Oregon: Timber Press, 1986. 302p. maps. bibliog.
This excellent book includes a well-researched chapter on the history of the island, orchid exploration, the various climatic zones and orchid habitats. Diagrams and

Flora and Fauna. Flora: general

photographs aid identification, and useful rainfall, temperature and humidity charts complete what is currently the definitive work on the subject.

74 **Carte internationale du tapis végétal et conditions écologique. Notice de la carte Madagascar.** (International map of vegetation cover and ecological conditions. Notes on the Madagascar map.)
Henri Humbert, G. Cours Darne.   Pondicherry, India: Section Scientifique et Technique d'Institut Français de Pondicherry, 1965. 160p. 3 maps.

Humbert's knowledge of the flora of Madagascar is unequalled. His many works on the subject were the result of thirty years' study and ten expeditions to Madagascar between 1912 and 1960. In 1927 he was responsible for establishing the country's first protected areas. The book accompanies three maps at a scale of 1:1,000,000. These maps are particularly interesting as they allow an appreciation of the changes in vegetation cover in the last thirty years.

75 **Flore de Madagascar et des Comores.**
Edited by Henri Humbert.   Paris: Muséum National d'Histoire Naturelle, 1936- .

This multi-volume series is the definitive work on the subject. 149 parts have been published to date, each describing a different family, and written by a specialist. The volume covering orchids has been translated (rather poorly) into English *Flora of Madagascar: orchids* by H. Perrier de la Bathie, translated by Steven D. Beckman. (California: Steven D. Beckman Publications, 1981).

76 **Flore et végétation de Madagascar.** (Flora and vegetation of Madagascar.)
J. Koechlin, J. L. Guillaumet, P. H. Morat.   Vaduz, Liechtenstein: J. Cramer, 1974. 687p. 23 maps.

A survey of the geography, geology, climate and subsequent effects of man on this long-isolated island-continent, allows the definition of twelve bioclimatic regions. The vegetation grouping of each region is closely related to the physical structure of the landscape, and is described and analysed in depth. This work is for biogeographers, ecologists and biologists concentrating on evolutionary mechanisms.

77 **Atlas des plantes ornementales et curieuses de Madagascar.** (Atlas of the ornamental and curious plants of Madagascar.)
M. Louvel.   Paris: Gouvernment General de Madagascar, 1931. 115p.

This is an atlas in size only; there are no maps but a collection of beautiful black-and-white photographs of trees in Madagascar which were exhibited at the International Colonial Exhibition in Paris. The author was the principal of the Department of Water and Forests in Madagascar. He has divided his selection into families, but he only chooses palms, aloes, and epiphytes. Palms predominate. This book is of more artistic than scientific interest.

78 **Madagascar: the unknown.**
May Moir, Goodale Moir. *The Orchid Review*, vol. 71, no. 837
(Mar. 1963), p. 68-73; no. 838 (Apr. 1963), p. 104-08.

Interesting as much for its picture of Madagascar shortly after independence as for its descriptions of the flora. Much of the author's time was spent in the rain forests which were far more extensive than today. They collected a large number of plants which would now be considered endangered and under strict protection.

79 **La végétation malgache.** (Malagasy vegetation.)
Henri Perrier de la Bathie.   Marseilles, France: Annales du Musée
Colonial de Marseille, 1921. 268p.

The author, a contemporary of Henri Humbert, made numerous visits to Madagascar, amassing a vast collection of plants and invertebrates which he donated to the natural history museum in Paris. His book is considered both the first and one of the most lucid explanations of man's effect on the landscape of Madagascar, and led to the creation of the first nature reserves in Madagascar in 1927. A later book by this author is *Biogéographie des plantes de Madagascar*. (Paris: Société d'Editions Géographique, Maritimes Coloniales, 1936. 156p). This describes the endemic vegetation by family, and the changes introduced by man are noted.

80 **Histoire particulière des plantes orchidées recueillies sur les trois îles australes d'Afrique.** (Special history of the orchids collected in the three southern islands of Africa.)
Aubert-Aubert du Petit-Thouars.   New York: Earl M. Coleman, 1979.
142p.

This is a reprint of a treatise first published in 1922 on the natural history of the orchids of Madagascar, Mauritius and Réunion. The author was one of the earliest botanical explorers of the islands and was fascinated by the endemism brought about by geographical isolation. The work contains an introduction to the orchid family, with two fold-out sheets containing a key to classification and identification, followed by detailed descriptions accompanied by 110 pages of botanical drawings. The reprint is accompanied by a historical introduction to the work in English, and a number of useful observations by Peter Goldblatt, Curator of African Botany at Missouri Botanic Garden.

81 **Crotalaria in Africa and Madagascar.**
R. M. Polhill.   Rotterdam, Netherlands: A. A. Balkema, 1982. 389p.

A complete, scientific account of the forty-two species of this legume which occur in Madagascar. The chemistry, cytology, breeding system and phytogeography are detailed.

82 **The succulent vegetation of Madagascar.**
Werner Rauh.   *Cactus and succulent journal*, no. 55 (1983), p. 124-27,
147-61, 201-08; no. 57 (1985), p. 99-102, 159-67, 217-19.

The author is the leading writer in this field. Other articles in the same journal are 'The genus Pachypodium', no. 44, (1972), p. 7-16, where he compares the African and Malagasy species and includes a large number of photographs; and 'The Xerophytic vegetation of southwestern Madagascar', no. 49 (1977), p. 99-103, 155-61, 197-204, 269-73; no. 50 (1978), p. 11-15, 55-59, 119-21, 159-65, 226-29, where he gives an overview of the plants that flourish in the dry conditions of the south-west.

83 **Mangroves of Africa and Madagascar.**
Alan Ward, Peter Bunyard.   Luxembourg: Office for Official
Publications of the European Community, 1992. 273p. maps. bibliog.
This work is based on a report of the same name, published in 1987 by J. M. Kramkimel and B. Bousquet, and updated by these authors for publication. It is written for a general audience, and begins with a description of the characteristics of mangroves along with factors affecting their conservation, such as agriculture. The second part are case histories, of which twelve pages are devoted to Madagascar.

84 **The baobab, Africa's upside-down tree.**
G. E. Wickens.   *Kew Bulletin*, vol. 37, no 2 (1982), p. 172-209.
A treatise on the African baobab, *Adansonia digitata* which also occurs in Madagascar, possibly introduced from Zanzibar. This is useful background reading to a genus with seven species in Madagascar.

Flora: medicinal plants

85 **Précis de matière medicale malgache.** (Precis of Malagasy medicinal material.)
Pierre Boiteau.   Antananarivo: Librairie de Madagascar, 1979. 80p.
A simply-produced small book, organized under different diseases and how to treat them with natural medicines. Recipes are included.

86 **Plantes médicinales malgaches.** (Malagasy medicinal plants.)
A. Descheemaeker.   Fianarantsoa, Madagascar: St Paul, 1990. 2nd ed. 112p.
This work is organized under diseases and includes three pages of black-and-white illustrations. It is not as comprehensive as *Précis de matière medicale malgache* (q.v.).

87 **Pharmacopee de l'Alaotra.** (Pharmacopoea of Alaotra.)
Zafera A. Rabesa.   Antananarivo: Tous Travaux, 1986. 290p.
Although this book only covers one area in the northern highlands it is very comprehensive, with many black-and-white illustrations of plants, each with an accompanying 'indication of therapy'. There are additional photographs of local people.

Fauna

88 **Nocturnal Malagasy primates: ecology, physiology and behaviour.**
P. Charles-Dominique, et al.   New York; London: Academic Press,
1980. 215p.
A series of scholarly descriptions by experts in their field on the nocturnal lemurs of
Madagascar.

89 **La faune malgache: son rôle dans les croyances et les usages indigènes.**
(The Malagasy fauna: its role in the beliefs and customs of the
indigenous people.)
Raymond Decary.   Paris: Payot, 1950. 187p. bibliog.
The author, a prolific writer on Madagascar with over 400 works to his name, here
provides a brief description of the fauna of the island and how it benefits or 'harms' the
local people as a source of food or taboo. He includes folklore, and legendary and
hypothetical animals. A fascinating book.

90 **Faune de Madagascar.** (Fauna of Madagascar.)
Tananarive: Office de la Recherche Scientifique et Technique Outre-
Mer; Paris: Centre National de la Recherche Scientifique, 1956- .
Sixty-four volumes have so far been published, and this was until recently the only
work to describe the entire spectrum of Malagasy fauna. It is still the most detailed,
and is considered the classic reference work. Each volume is by a different author or
authors, specialists in their field. Volume 35 deals with birds; volumes 33, 36, and 47
cover reptiles; and volume 13 is zoogeography. Thirty-eight volumes are devoted to
invertebrates.

91 **Field guide to the mammals of Africa including Madagascar.**
T. Haltenorth, H. Diller, translated by Robert W. Hayman.   London:
Collins, 1980. 400p.
This book is useful in that it is portable and depicts most mammals, but the
illustrations are not accurate enough for field identification.

92 **Lemurs of Madagascar and the Comoros.**
Caroline Harcourt.   Gland, Switzerland; Cambridge, England:
International Union for the Conservation of Nature, 1990. 240p. maps.
(IUCN Red Data Book).
One of a series of Red Data Books compiled by the World Conservation Monitoring
Centre providing information on endangered species. Black-and-white photographs
accompany each species description, which includes distribution, population, habitat
and ecology, threats, conservation measures, and captive breeding. The lemur's
category as a threatened species is noted, ranging from endangered and rare to
abundant. Maps showing distribution accompany the text and a detailed list of
references is provided on each species.

Flora and Fauna. Fauna

93 **Guide to the birds of Madagascar.**
Olivier Langrand, illustrated by Vincent Bretagnolle. New Haven,
Connecticut; London: Yale University Press, 1990. 364p. maps. bibliog.
About fifty per cent of Madagascar's bird species are endemic, and this excellent field
guide is an essential aid to identification. There are forty colour plates and the detailed
descriptions include local names, behaviour, voice, habitat, diet and distribution. Of
additional interest to ornithologists is *The endemic birds of Madagascar,* by T. J. Dee.
(Cambridge, England: International Council for Bird Preservation, 1986. 173p.).
There are no illustrations but the bibliography gives it value for those seeking highly
specialized bird references.

94 **Chameleons.**
James Martin, with photographs by Art Wolfe. New York: Facts on
File; London: Blandford, 1992. 176p. bibliog.
This is the first serious work devoted solely to chameleons, and the author has
provided everything the chameleon aficionado could wish for. Two-thirds of the
world's species of this lizard are found in Madagascar, including both the largest and
smallest. This book begins with a description of chameleon anatomy and behaviour,
then details four in-depth case studies showing adaptation to various environments,
from desert to rain forest. Finally there is a summary of all known species with
scientific and English names, description and distribution, and a very useful
bibliography. The writing is lively, and superb colour photographs add to the book's
appeal.

95 **A new species of Hapalemur (primate) from south-east Madagascar.**
B. Meier, R. Albignac, A. Peyrieras, Y. Rumpler, P. Wright. *Folia
Primatologia*, vol. 48 (1987), p. 211-15.
The first account of the discovery and identification of the golden bamboo lemur,
Hapalemur aureus.

96 **Lemurs of Madagascar. An action plan for their conservation 1993-1999.**
Compiled by Russell A. Mittermeier, William R. Konstant, Martin E.
Nicoll, Olivier Langrand. Gland, Switzerland: International Union for
the Conservation of Nature, IUCN/SSC Primate Specialist Group, 1992.
58p. maps.
This study is divided into six sections. After a general introduction to the lemurs and
their endangered status, it looks at protected areas and sites of special biological
importance by geographical region. Lemur taxa are divided into highest priority, high
priority and priority, and conservation measures proposed. The sixth section is the
budget for the Lemur Action Plan.

97 **Animal lifestyles and anatomies: the case of the prosimian primates.**
Charles Oxnard, Robin Crompton, Susan Lieberman. Seattle,
Washington; London: University of Washington Press, 1990. 174p.
bibliog.
Three primatologists pose the question 'To what extent are the structures of animals
related to their ways of life and vice versa?' Using video, film and field studies they
have drawn up a detailed account, with numerous schematic diagrams, of the

behaviour of every species of prosimian, most of which are lemurs. The purpose is to make possible predictions about the life-styles of extinct species from the anatomies of their fossilized remains, and conversely predict the anatomies of very rare species from their life-styles.

98 **Behavioral variation: case study of a Malagasy lemur.**
Alison Richard.   Lewisburg, Pennsylvania: Bucknell University Press; London: Associated Universities Press, 1978. 213p. bibliog.

This scholarly study features the sifaka lemur, *Propithecus verreauxi* which lives in a wide variety of habitats throughout the island. The author, an anthropologist who has done extensive field work in Madagascar, investigates the effects of environment on the social organization of the animals, based on four groups in different areas and during different seasons.

99 **Weasels, civets, mongooses and their relatives. An action plan for the conservation of mustelids and viverrids.**
A. Schreiber, R. Wirth, M. Riffel, H. Van Rompaey.   Gland, Switzerland: International Union for the Conservation of Nature, IUCN/SSC Mustelid and Viverrid Specialist Group, 1989. 100p. maps.

Madagascar's unique fauna includes eight species of Viverridae. This action plan looks at the threats facing these two families of mammals worldwide, as well as in Madagascar. Chapter 4: 'Accounts of mustelids and viverrids known or likely to be threatened' includes a distribution map and photograph of each of the Malagasy carnivores, and gives information on their status in the wild and in captivity, their occurrence in protected areas and recommended actions for their conservation. The same organization has made a similar report of the insectivores in *African insectivora and elephant-shrews. An action plan for their conservation*, by Martin Nicoll, Galen Rathbun. (Gland, Switzerland: International Union for the Conservation of Nature, IUCN/SSC Insectivore, Tree-shrew and Elephant-shrew Specialist Group, 1990. 53p.). Chapter 2 covers the *Tenrecidae* of Madagascar, dividing the country into biogeographical regions, followed by species in particular need of conservation.

100 **Madagascar ornithology: Malagasy birds.**
James Sibree.   Antananarivo: London Missionary Society Press, 1889. 79p.

The great 19th-century observer of all things Malagasy has here provided a work of much interest to present-day readers, although the list and descriptions are inevitably limited. The strength of the book is in the accounts of Malagasy folklore and taboos associated with birds. The book is reprinted from the Antananarvio Annual.

101 **Lemur biology.**
Edited by Ian Tattersall, Robert W. Sussman.   New York: Plenum, 1975. 365p. maps. bibliogs.

Many contributors have built up this work which focuses on the anatomy, behaviour and ecology of several species of lemur. It stresses the importance of prosimians such as lemurs in our understanding of evolution and social behaviour, and includes an analysis of the research carried out on lemurs up to the mid-1970s.

102 **Madagascar's lemurs.**
Ian Tattersall. *Scientific American*, vol. 268, no. 1 (Jan. 1993),
p. 90-97.

The author continues his evaluation of the importance of lemur studies in the understanding of the evolution of man. He makes some interesting comparisons between lemurs, the so-called lower primates, and higher primates, the anthropoid apes and human beings. He concludes that the behaviour of lemurs gives us important clues to the behaviour of primates in the Eocene epoch. The extinctions caused by man of about fourteen species of lemur, and the continuing threat to the surviving species is also discussed.

103 **The primates of Madagascar.**
Ian Tattersall. New York; Guildford, England: Columbia University
Press, 1981. 382p. maps. bibliog.

The author, a primatologist, is recognized as one of the world authorities on lemurs. This is the most comprehensive book to date on their biology. It catalogues all the species of lemur known at that time, with a detailed environmental account of Madagascar and a history of lemur studies from the early explorers to the end of the 1970s.

Biogeography and ecology in Madagascar.
See item no. 21.

Three visits to Madagascar during the years 1853-1854-1856.
See item no. 132.

Madagascar, an historical and descriptive account of the island and its former dependencies
See item no. 135.

Madagascar before the conquest: the island, the country, and the people.
See item no. 140.

Hanitriniala.
See item no. 322.

Coral reefs and coastal zone of Toliara: bibliography.
See item no. 340.

Madagascan orchids: an annotated bibliography.
See item no. 341.

History

General

104 Madagascar rediscovered.
Mervyn Brown. London: Damien Tunnacliffe, 1978. 310p. 9 maps. bibliog.

This history from early times to independence is a well-informed, and highly readable account by an ex-British Ambassador. The most accurate, comprehensive and enjoyable of the modern histories, especially strong on the pre-colonial period. A new edition is expected early 1994. This will greatly expand the section on the colonial period and add four chapters on the post-independence history up to the inauguration of the Third Republic in 1993. This substantial new material will provide the most complete account of the history of Madagascar in the 20th century.

105 Histoire de Madagascar. (History of Madagascar.)
Hubert Deschamps. Paris: Berger-Levrault. 1965, 348p.

This is the best of the French histories, covering the period from the first human arrivals to independence with useful summaries of the economy and the culture of the Malagasy. Sub-headings within the chapters, and the author's clear style make it easy to read.

106 Madagascar in history: essays from the 1970s.
Edited by Raymond K. Kent. Albany, California: Foundation for Malagasy Studies, 1979. 354p. bibliog.

There are thirteen contributions, seven translated from French by the editor. History is widely interpreted to include archaeology, ethnology, and sociology. The authors include many of the leading academic authorities: French; American; British; and Malagasy.

107 **Omaly sy anio (hier et aujourd'hui).** (Yesterday and today.)
Antananarivo: Université de Madagascar, 1975-84. 9 vols.

These volumes are reviews of historical studies, many of them presented at seminars organized by the university. They are mainly in French, but some are in English and some in Malagasy. Each paper has a summary in the other languages. The series contains much of the best modern scholarship on the history of the island in its various aspects.

108 **Histoire de Madagascar.** (History of Madagascar.)
Édouard Ralaimihoatra.   Antananarivo: La Librairie de Madagascar, 1982. 289p.

A well-written political narrative history by a Malagasy scholar who was Chancellor of the Académie malgache. While devoting most of its pages to the Merina kingdom, there are useful accounts of the history and dynasties of the other main ethnic groups. The final part, on the 20th century up to the achievement of autonomy in 1958, is a reasonably objective account of the achievements and problems of French colonial rule and the rise of nationalism. There is some useful information on administration and social organization, but not much about the economy.

109 **The Malagasy Republic: Madagascar today.**
Virginia Thompson, Richard Adloff.   Stanford, California: Stanford University Press, 1965. 504p. map. bibliog.

After a sketchy overview of pre-colonial history and a larger section on French rule the authors concentrate on the political status of Madagascar just after independence. The second (and larger) section is particularly valuable for its great detail on education, religion, literature and the information media, rural economy, transportation, finance, industry, trade and labour in the early 1960s. It gives a clear picture of the relative prosperity of Madagascar before the impact of 'revolutionary socialism'.

Archaeology and pre-19th century

110 **Historical traditions and the foundations of monarchy in Imerina.**
Gerald M. Berg.   Ann Arbor, Michigan: University of Michigan, 1975. 388p. maps. bibliog.

This is an enormously detailed Ph D thesis, but it is written in straightforward language and is easy to read. The author discusses the mysterious Vazimba, early inhabitants of Madagascar, who feature in the myths and legends of the Merina/Hova people. One version is that there were originally two groups of people: the Vazimba who were short, dark skinned, with crinkly hair, and were considered inferior, and the Hova who were light-skinned and superior. The alternative view is that the Vazimba were not a separate race but were direct ancestors of the Hova. These two theories are discussed in the light of archeological findings and other evidence to explain the dominance of the Hova culture.

111   **Collection des oeuvrages anciens concernant Madagascar.** (A collection
of ancient works concerning Madagascar.)
Alfred Grandidier, Henri Freidevaux, Guillaume Grandidier.   Paris:
Comité de Madagascar, 1903-10. 9 vols.

An extraordinary achievement by the renowned explorer and naturalist, Alfred
Grandidier. Guillaume, his son, and Henri Freidevaux assisted but these volumes are
largely Alfred's work. They are a collection of all the known writings on Madagascar
from 1500 to 1800. Though some originals were written in French, many have been
translated from Portuguese, Spanish, Dutch, English, German, Italian and Latin.
Volume 1 covers the period from 1500 to 1613, volume 2 from 1613 to 1640, volume 3
from 1640 to 1716, volume 4 contains the translation of *Robert Drury's journal* (q.v.),
volumes 5 and 6 cover the period from 1718 to 1800, volume 7 covers some further
works from 1604 to 1658, volumes 8 and 9 are mainly devoted to Flacourt's two
volumes of history.

112   **Dating of modified femora of extinct dwarf hippopotamus from southern
Madagascar.**
R. D. E. MacPhee, D. A. Burney.   *Journal of Archaeological Science*,
vol. 18, no. 6 (Nov. 1991), p. 695-707.

Two significant events in the early history of Madagascar were the arrival of man and
the loss of nearly two dozen species of land vertebrates in 'subfossil extinctions'. The
consensus is that the extinctions occurred shortly after human arrival which was
thought to have occurred between 300 and 500 AD. Examination of the bones of the
extinct dwarf hippopotamus found in south-west Madagascar shows signs of butchering
by man-made tools. Since the bones have been dated to between 2,100 and 1,900 years
ago, the arrival of man now appears to be have been several hundred years earlier than
previously supposed. The authors debate the relevance to the 'Blitzkrieg' theory of
extinction that is linked to human intervention.

113   **An ancient account of Madagascar.**
Hieronymus Megiserus.   In: *From Fianarantsoa to Ikongo*. George A.
Shaw.   Tananarive: Friend's Foreign Mission Association, 1877.
p. 23-52.

A foreword by James Sibree introduces one of the oldest accounts of Madagascar,
originally published in 1609 in Altenbourg, Germany, under the title *Beschreibung der
Moechtigen und weitberuehmten Insel Madagascar*. The translation has been incorporated into Shaw's travelogue, presumably to widen the historical perspective.
Megiserus describes his book on the title page as 'A genuine, thorough, and ample, as
well as historical and chronological description of the exceedingly rich, powerful and
famous island of Madagascar called also St Lawrence; together with an account of all
its qualities, peculiarities, inhabitants, animals, fruits, and vegetables, also a history of
what has happened there before and since its discovery'. He shows some scepticism
over Marco Polo's description of the Roc, but inaccurately lists elephants and camels
among the 'strange creatures' that live there. However, his description of the ring-
tailed lemur is instantly recognisable.

114 **Urban origins in eastern Africa. Proceedings of the 1989 Madagascar workshop.**
Edited by Paul Sinclair, Jean Aimé Rakotoarisoa. Stockholm: Central Board of National Antiquities, 1989.

These papers are mainly in French, but there are two in English: 'Societies in Madagascar: case studies in cultural diversification' by T. Wright and J. Rakotoarisoa (p. 21-30); and 'Regional archaeological survey in Avarodrano' by S. Kus & T. Wright (p. 68-78). The former discusses excavations in different climatic areas: Mananara, a forested area on the north-east coast; Androy, semi-desert in the south-east; and the old highland kingdom of Imerina. The latter examines Avarondrano which is the north-eastern quadrant of Imerina, an area which includes the ancient towns of Ambohimanga and Ambohidrabiby. Copies are available from P.O. Box 5405, S-11484, Stockholm, Sweden.

115 **The African element in Madagascar.**
Pierre Vérin. *Anzania*, vol. 11 (1976).

The author, an archaeologist, here discusses the different theories on early immigration to Madagascar. His findings indicate that people of African origin, mainly Bantu speaking, probably arrived in Madagascar during the 9th century. Immigration continued until the 16th century.

116 **The history of civilisation in north Madagascar.**
Pierre Vérin, translated from the French by David Smith. Rotterdam, Netherlands; Boston: A. A. Balkema, 1986. 431p. maps. bibliog.

A scholarly study of the various civilizations which have succeeded one another along the coastal area of northern Madagascar between Maintirano in the west and Cape Masoala in the east. The author is an archaeologist who has worked for many years in Madagascar. From his excavations of the area he surveys the period between the 9th and 19th centuries, providing a historical review of the civilization of the region where Islamized peoples from east Africa came to settle alongside the original Malagasy inhabitants. This is an important book on the prehistory of Madagascar.

Pirates

117 **The Madagascar pirates.**
F. D. Arnold-Forster. New York: Lothrop, Lee & Shepard, 1957. 252p. bibliog.

This straightforward book was probably written for young people. It presents the lives of the Madagascar pirates: John Avery, Samuel Burgess, John Halsey, Nathaniel North and Thomas White.

118   **A general history of the pyrates.**
Daniel Defoe, edited by Manuel Schonhorn.   London: Dent, 1972.
695p.

Originally published in two volumes in 1724 and 1728 under the title 'A general history of the robberies and murders of the most notorious pyrates', under the pseudonym 'Captain Charles Johnson' (London: [n.p.]), this is the classic work on pirates. This modern edition has been edited, updated and annotated, and illustrated with contemporary engravings. Defoe spent many years gathering information from accounts of voyages, conversations with ships' captains, and reports of pirates' trials. The only time Defoe's imagination seems to have got the better of him is in the description of the pirates' Republic of Libertalia, established in the bay of Diego Suarez. This is fiction. Pirates who worked the coasts of Madagascar, such as Captain Avery and Captain Kidd are described in the first eleven chapters of volume 2. Madagascar was referred to by Defoe as 'Magadoxa'.

119   **Les pirates à Madagascar.** (The pirates of Madagascar.)
Hubert Deschamps.   Paris: Berger-Levrault, 1949. 238p.

This is the most thorough and best-written account of piracy in Madagascar. It is the standard work, drawing from a variety of sources but mainly Defoe, although the author accepts as fact the fictional account of Libertalia.

120   **A compendious history of the Indian Wars with an account of the rise, progress, strength and forces of Angria the pyrate. . . with an account of the life and actions of John Plantain, a notorious pyrate at Madagascar; his wars with the natives of that island.**
Clement Downing.   London: T. Cooper, 1737. 238p.

The section dealing with Madagascar is a bloodthirsty and somewhat fanciful account of the actions of John Plantain, said to be the inspiration for Long John Silver. He was born in Jamaica of English parents, and boarded a pirate ship bound for Madagascar as a young man. During his time there he declared himself king of 'Ranter-Bay' (Rantabé) on the east coast opposite the pirate stronghold of Isle Sainte Marie. This account, though lacking in hard facts, gives some useful insights into the pirates' way of life.

121   **Pirates of the eastern seas (1618-1723).**
Charles Grey.   London: Sampson Low, Marston, 1933. 336p.

The author drew his information mainly from the archives of the East India Company, so the viewpoint of this work is largely Anglo-Indian. There is one chapter specifically on the pirate settlements of Madagascar, and many of the pirate adventures described take place in or around Madagascar.

The 19th century

122 **Raombana: l'historien. 1809-1855.** (Raombana: the historian.
1809-1855.)
Simon Ayache.   Fianarantsoa, Madagascar: Ambozontany, 1976.
510p.

An outstanding work by a former professor of history at Antananarivo University. His
subject is Raombana, an extraordinary Malagasy historian who had been educated in
Britain and wrote in English, see his *Histoires* (q.v.). Ayache intended this book to be
an introduction to and commentary on his scholarly editions of all Raombana's
writings, but so far only volume 1 of the History has been published as funding for the
Annals and Journal was not available.

123 **Le meurtre de Radama II.** (The assassination of Radama II.)
Père Adrien Boudou.   France: Pilot de la Beaujardière, 1938. 60p.
(Mémoires de l'Académie malgache, Fascicule 26).

King Radama II was assassinated in 1863, strangled with a silken cord, since it was
taboo to shed royal blood. This is a study of the events surrounding his death by the
historian of the Jesuit mission in Madagascar, quoting and commenting on
contemporary documents from Jesuit and other sources. A substantial section is
devoted to refuting contemporary accusations by Jesuits and other French sources that
William Ellis, of the London Missionary Society, was responsible for Radama's death.
Some Malagasy believe Radama survived the strangulation. This theory is set out in
Radama II: prince de la renaissance malgache 1861-1863 (q.v.).

124 **Histoire des rois (Tantaran' ny Andriana).** (History of the kings.)
Père Callet, translated by G. S. Chapus, E. Ratsimba.   Paris: Editions
de la Librairie de Madagascar, 1974. 3 vols.

The oral history of the Merina kings, from their mythical origins, was collected by
Father Callet for the Académie malgache. This vast and invaluable collection has been
adequately translated from the original Malagasy. Its usefulness is enhanced by the
companion work by Delivré, *L'histoire des rois d'Imerina* (q.v.).

125 **Rainilaiarivony: un homme d'état malgache.** (Rainilaiarivony: a
Malagasy statesman.)
G. S. Chapus, G. Mondain.   Paris: Dilontremer, 1953. 452p.

A comprehensive biography of Madagascar's long-term prime minister who retained
his power by marrying three queens in succession. The book contains much detail of
the period (1828-1897) and provides some excellent insights into the lives and customs
of the royal household and the leading political families.

126 **A history of the island of Madagascar.**
Samuel Copland.   London: Burton & Smith. 1822. 368p.

Subtitled 'Comprising a political account of the island, the religion, manners and
customs of its inhabitants and its natural productions with an appendix containing a
history of the several attempts to introduce Christianity into the Island'. The author
had no first-hand knowledge of Madagascar and the book is an entertaining collection
of inaccuracies and pomposities. Much of his source material came from Flacourt, but

he takes a strongly anti-French stance. He plunges into the natural history section with vigour, describing, for example, a bison with 'very large horns, the points of which are wide enough apart for three men to sit between them'. Some descriptions may be from early accounts of now-extinct lemurs: 'The baboon grows to an enormous size. . . at least seven feet high when standing on its back legs'.

127   **L'île Nosy Be de Madagascar: histoire d'une colonisation.** (The island of Nosy Be: history of a colonization.)
Raymond Decary.   Paris: Éditions Maritimes et d'Outre-mer, 1960. 225p. bibliog.
Nosy Be was the first French possession in Madagascar. This is a detailed description of the island and its inhabitants at the time of the annexation in 1841, written by a member of the Colonial Office in the 1920s and 1930s who has contributed much to our knowledge of Madagascar.

128   **L'histoire des rois d'Imerina: inteprétation d'une tradition orale.** (The history of the kings of Imerina: interpretation of an oral tradition.)
Alain Delivré.   Paris: Klincksieck, 1974. 448p.
The author interprets and comments on the three volume work by Callet, *Histoire des rois* (q.v.).

129   **Radama II: prince de la renaissance malgache 1861-1863.** (Radama II: prince of the Malagasy renaissance 1861-1863.)
Raymond Delval.   Paris: Editions de l'École, 1972. 960p. maps. bibliog.
King Radama II reigned for only two years before being assassinated. This well-researched book is a full biography with a very detailed account of the political background amounting to a history of Madagascar in the first half of the 19th century. The author supports the theory that Radama II survived strangulation (a belief held by many Malagasy) and lived in hiding in the remote area south of Majunga for many years. Despite its length this is a very readable account of a fascinating story.

130   **History of Madagascar.**
Rev. William Ellis.   London: Fisher, Son & Co; Paris: Quai de l'École, 1838. 2 vols. map.
The author was the foreign secretary to the London Missionary Society (LMS), and these two volumes, based on the LMS archives, are considered the standard text on the early work of the British missionaries, and the history of Madagascar from 1818 to 1837, when the missionaries were compelled to withdraw owing to the hostility of Queen Ranavalona I. The first 200 pages comprise a well-written summary of the previous history of Madagascar as it was known at that time. The book is nicely illustrated with fifteen etchings and a fine 'Baxter print' (hand-painted etching) as a frontispiece of volume 1 showing Rafaralahy, governor of Foule Pointe.

131   **Madagascar revisited.**
Rev. William Ellis.   London: John Murray, 1867. 502p. map.
The book is subtitled: 'Describing the events of a new reign and the revolution which followed'. The new reign was that of King Radama II, when missionaries were

readmitted into Madagascar; and the revolution was the acceptance of freedom of religion in the country, which was formally declared in a treaty with England in 1865. Ellis revisited Madagascar in 1862. His main aim was to build a series of Martyr Memorial Churches to commemmorate the Christians who lost their lives during the cruel reign of King Radama's mother, Queen Ranavalona. Ellis became the unofficial advisor of King Radama II, and was involved in competition with the French Jesuits for influence in the royal court. He provides a remarkable eye-witness account of events leading to the overthrow and murder of Radama II.

132 **Three visits to Madagascar during the years 1853-1854-1856.**
Rev. William Ellis.   London: John Murray, 1858. 476p. maps.

Subtitled: 'Including a journey to the capital with notices of the natural history of the country and the present civilisation of the people'. During the first two visits he only got as far as Tamatave, being refused permission to continue to Antananarivo. He succeeded in 1856, stayed a month, and was granted a formal audience with Queen Ranavalona, for whom he had a message from the British Foreign Secretary. A further purpose of his visit was to establish contact with secret Christians and to give them Bibles. Ellis was a keen botanist who made careful notes on species of orchids collected and learned what he could of the fauna. Although his description of people and way of life is necessarily circumspect, Europeans being subjected to hostility, he still provides a fascinating insight into Madagascar in the mid-19th century. Part of the book is taken up with descriptions of South Africa and other Indian Ocean islands. It is beautifully illustrated with etchings.

133 **Histoire du royaume Hova.** (History of the Hova kingdom.)
Le Reverend Père Malzac.   Tananarive: Imprimerie Catholique, 1930. 645p.

A compendious history of the Merina kingdom, from its origins in the 18th century to 1897 when it was assimilated into French colonial Madagascar. The author is a Jesuit with an inevitable French-Catholic bias.

134 **Madagascar and the Malagasy.**
Samuel P. Oliver.   London: Day & Son, [1865?]. 105p. map.

The book is subtitled: 'Sketches in the provinces of Tamatave, Betanimena and Ankova'. The sketches are both literary and artistic, the author being a member of the Royal Academy of Art. As a young lieutenant, Oliver was ADC to General Johnstone, Commander-in-Chief in Mauritius, who led a British Government mission to Antananarivo in 1862 to present a letter of congratulations and gifts from Queen Victoria on the occasion of the coronation of Radama II and the reopening of Madagascar to foreign trade. The book is an account of the journey and the stay in the capital. It provides a good picture of the royal court and its circle, and is an enjoyable read. It is beautifully illustrated with the author's tinted lithographs.

135 **Madagascar, an historical and descriptive account of the island and its former dependencies.**
Samuel P. Oliver.   London; New York: Macmillan, 1886. 2 vols. maps.

An excellent and thorough description of all aspects of the island, drawing on the work of his contemporaries for specialized information. Volume 1 covers history up to 1883, geography, topography, climatology, geology and natural history. Volume 2 has natural and agricultural products, ethnology, manufactured goods, administration, trade and revenue, currency, weights and measures; bibliography and cartography; and a detailed account of the Franco-Malagasy war of 1883-1885. The book is easy to use with clear margin headings indicating subjects, and some excellent pull-out maps.

136 **Notre unité et l'époque colonial.** (Our unity and the colonial period.)
Jacques Rabemananjara. *Présence Africaine*, 1956, 16p.
This is a paper presented to the First International Conference of Negro Writers and Artists. It is an analysis of the pre-colonial period and the consequences of the French threat to the unity of the Malagasy, leading to the creation of different local political movements.

137 **Journal d'un malgache du XIX siecle: le livre de Rakotovao, 1843-1906.**
(Diary of a Malagasy of the 19th century: the book of Rakotovao, 1843-1906.)
Rakotovao, translated by Annick Cohen-Bessy. Paris: L'Harmattan, 1991. 2 vols. (Series Repères pour Madagascar et l'Ocean Indien).
Life in Madagascar in the 19th century has been well chronicled by British (and to a lesser degree French) writers, but there are very few accounts written by the Malagasy. The diarist describes the day-to-day life in Imerina. As one of the early converts to Christianity he observes the religious life of the period and events in the Royal Court, as well as witnessing the French Wars which preceded French colonization.

138 **Histoires.** (Histories.)
Raombana. Antananarivo: l'Académie malgache, 1980. 304p.
Raombana was one of twins sent to England for six years in the early 19th century by King Radama. On his return to Madagascar he became private secretary to Queen Ranavalona I and during that period kept a diary in English. This work is a unique record of pre-colonial Madagascar, all the more extraordinary in that it was written by a Malagasy in English. There is a French translation on the opposite pages. The book should be studied along with the commentary by Ayache, *Raombana: l'historien. 1809-1855* (q.v.).

139 **Remarks on slavery in Madagascar.**
Joseph S. Sewell. London: Elliot Stock, 1876. 40p.
The export of slaves from Madagascar was officially abolished in 1820 in a treaty between Radama I and Britain. However, internal slavery continued until it was ended by the French conquerors in 1896. The author, a member of the Friends' Foreign Mission, delivered an address denouncing slavery shortly before leaving the island, leading to him in turn being denounced by the furious prime minister, who at that time held the reins of power. The booklet is in two parts: the address; and remarks on the address. The comments on the nature of slavery in Madagascar are illuminating. Sewell points out that it was very different from the plantation slavery in America or the West Indies, that the slaves were at liberty to leave, although few had anywhere to go, and they could take jobs for other employers, although their master was entitled to his cut of their wage. But the cruelty to the slaves is also highlighted.

140 **Madagascar before the conquest: the island, the country, and the people.**
James Sibree. London: T. Fisher Unwin, 1896. 382p. maps.
The author was one of the notable documenters of Madagascar in the second half of
the 19th century, with an interesting and fluid writing style. Like many of the
missionaries, he had a keen eye for the natural history and ethnology of the island,
with an unusual lack of paternalism. His love of Madagascar and its people seems
genuine, and he is particularly good on folklore, legends and customs. His chapter on
the funeral ceremonies of the different tribes is very rewarding. Much of the book is
translated from Grandidier's works. It is illustrated by early photographs which makes
it interesting to the present-day visitor.

141 **Études sur le règne de Radama Ier 1810-1828.** (Studies of the reign of
Radama I 1810-1828.)
Jean Valette. Antananarivo: Imprimerie Nationale, 1962. 84p.
Though short, this is the best available study of the important reign of Radama I,
based mainly on the National Archives of the Malagasy Republic and the publications
of the Académie malgache. It recounts the main achievements of Radama with the
help of British agents and missionaries: the abolition of the slave trade; education;
changes in laws and customs; and the establishment of a written language. Half the
book deals with the military expansion of the Merina kingdom, and an appendix
quotes descriptions of Radama by contemporary European travellers.

142 **Black odyssey: John L. Waller and the promise of American life.**
Randall B. Woods. Lawrence, Kansas: Regents Press, 1981. 254p.
A biography of John Waller, a former slave who, after an active political career in
Kansas, became one of the first black American diplomats, serving as consul in
Madagascar from 1891-93. His involvement in the local politics, supporting the
Malagasy Government against the encroachments of the French, led to his dismissal by
the State Department, but he stayed on in Madagascar to promote a plan to establish
an Afro-American community in Fort Dauphin. When the French invaded Madagascar
they took Waller prisoner and sentenced him to 10 years hard labour, an incident that
strained the relations between France and the USA.

War and revolt against France (1883-1899)

143 **Two campaigns; Madagascar and Ashantee.**
Bennet Burleigh. London: Fisher Unwin, 1896. 372p.
Burleigh was war correspondent to the *Daily Telegraph* between 1894 and 1895. His
account of the 'campaign' which led to the island becoming a French colony is well-
written and fills the gaps left by the other British war correspondent, E. F. Knight in
Madagascar in war time (q.v.).

144   **The rising of the red shawls: a revolt in Madagascar, 1895-1899.**
Stephen Ellis.   Cambridge, England; New York: Cambridge
University Press, 1985. 214p. bibliog. (African Studies Series 43).
An important and illuminating account of a key event in the modern history of
Madagascar. Rebellion broke out a few months after the French military invasion of
1895 brought about the downfall of the Merina monarchy. The *menalamba* (red
shawls) rebellion, which takes its name from the red earth-stained white shawls of the
Malagasy, lasted three years. The author has done some unique research, having
learned Malagasy in order to study archive material. In a clear, readable style he
focuses on the causes, progress and consequences of the rebellion in Imerina.

145   **Madagascar in war time.**
E. F. Knight.   London; New York; Bombay: Longmans; Green, 1896.
336p.
An account by the special correspondent of *The Times* describing his time among the
Hova tribe (now known as the Merina) during the French invasion of 1895. He
provides an excellent account of the campaign and the assault on Antananarivo which
he witnessed. This is an elegantly written and interesting account by a phlegmatic
Victorian gentleman doing the 'right thing' in the face of barbarism and rampant
dishonesty. He describes a time when each village was ruled by a 'king', mostly robber
kings. He is especially interesting – and probably accurate – in his coverage of the
southern tribes who encouraged the fighting between their two enemies, the French
and the Hova.

146   **Five years in Madagascar. With notes on the military situation.**
Col. Francis Cornwallis Maude.   London: Chapman & Hall, 1895.
285p. map.
This is an entertaining collection of personal impressions of life in Madagascar during
the last years of the monarchy, much of it concerned with, and justifying, French
attempts to establish a protectorate over the island. There are some useful descriptions
and comments on the royal court and the elderly prime minister's vain attempts to
keep the French at bay. Contrast is provided by the author's experiences of running a
timber company in Maroantsetra, and there are some notes on slavery, which was still
commonplace.

147   **Madagascar and France.**
George Shaw.   London: Religious Tract Society, 1885. Reprinted,
New York: Negro Universities Press, 1969. 320p.
The author was a British missionary who was arrested in Tamatave by the invading
French forces in 1883, on suspicion of trying to poison French troops. He was kept
prisoner for nearly two months. The incident, which aroused strong anti-French feeling
in Britain, is the centrepiece of the book which also contains descriptions of the island,
the people, and the flora and fauna, along with some historical background.

148   **The Shervingtons, soldiers of fortune.**
Kathleen Shervington.   London, T. Fisher Unwin, 1899. 280p.
Of the three Shervingtons whose exploits are described here, it was the father, Colonel
Charles Robert St Leger Shervington, who was concerned with Madagascar. Having

served in the Zulu wars, he came to the island in 1884 as a mercenary to help the Merina monarchy in their fight against French rule, although he seems to have been mainly on good terms with the French. He returned to Madagascar in 1894 to help train the Malagasy army in preparation for the French invasion in the following year, but, finding his advice ignored, left the island shortly after the campaign began. This is rather a dull book but there are some insights into Malagasy life just before the French conquest.

Colonial period (1895-1960)

149 **Chez les Hova.** (With the Hova.)
Jean Carol.   Paris: Paul Ollendorff, 1898. 431p.
Jean Carol was the pseudonym of Gabriel Laffaille, the director of the printing press in Antananarivo. His book is an in-depth study of the Hova (Merina) peoples of the highlands written from the viewpoint of an unusually liberal Frenchman. Of particular interest is his account of events in the first years of French rule, in which he is strongly critical of Governor-General Gallieni for his humiliation of the Queen and for the judicial murder of two leading Malagasy in 1896.

150 **Madagascar pendant la première guerre mondiale.** (Madagascar during the First World War.)
Maurice Gontard.   Tananarive: Société malgache d'Edition. [n.d.] 130p. bibliog.
There is little on Madagascar's role in the First World War so this is a useful book. The author has collected and considered all aspects of his subject, using archive material. Madagascar made an important contribution to the war, with 'volunteers' recruited to aid the Allied effort, and the country helped to fill the demand for raw materials. The war precipitated economic development and highlighted weaknesses in Madagascar's infrastructure.

151 **L'insurrection malgache de 1947.** (The Malagasy uprising of 1947.)
Jacques Tronchon.   Fianarantsoa, Madagascar: Editions Ambozontany Fianarantsoa; Paris: Karthala, 1986. 400p. 3 maps.
The author is a Franciscan friar who has worked for many years in Madagascar. His book details the events and participants of the nationalist rebellion which broke out on March 29, 1947, and took two years, and the loss of some 80,000 lives, to subdue. It is a comprehensive account including an analysis of its causes and clarification of responsibility.

The Second World War

152 The blood red island.
Rupert Croft-Cooke. London; New York: Staples Press, 1953.
248p.

The author was Field Security Officer with the British invading forces of 1942, and took part in the landing at Diego Suarez and in most of the rest of the campaign. This is an often amusing, lively, readable, and journalistic account of the campaign and of the author's own adventures.

153 Into Madagascar.
Kenneth C. Gandar Dower. Hammondsworth, England; New York: Penguin, 1943. 112p.

A racy, amusing, and personal account of the British invasion and occupation of Madagascar in 1942. The author was with the Kings African Rifles, and endearingly quotes James Thurber 'Don't get it right, get it written'. Nevertheless it seems a fairly accurate account of events and he is honest enough not to include the initial landing at Diego Suarez, since he was not there.

154 The King's African Rifles in Madagascar.
Kenneth C. Gandar Dower. Nairobi: C. S. I. Ministry of Information, [n.d.] 68p. 2 maps.

This is a propaganda booklet for the soldiers who fought in Madagascar during the British invasion; an edition was also produced in Swahili. It was privately distributed, so as not to offend the French. It sets out clearly and with many photographs the role of the King's African Rifles during the invasion, and has particularly helpful maps showing the military operations.

155 Hands to play.
Laurence Grafftey-Smith. London; Boston, Massachusetts: Routledge & Kegan Paul, 1975. 212p.

An autobiography with one chapter on the British occupation of Madagascar in 1942. The author was sent by the Foreign Office as advisor to the Commander of the British Forces in Madagascar.

156 Hitler's plan for Madagascar.
Eugene Hevesi. New York: American Jewish Committee, 1941. 14p.

This is extracted from the *Contemporary Jewish Record*, (1941), p. 381-93. The author points out that from as early as the 1920s Madagascar had attracted attention as a possible dumping ground for unwanted European citizens: in 1926 the Polish government considered settling a large number of peasants there, followed a decade later by a Polish mission with the aim of the forced settlement of Polish Jews on the island. The Nazis then looked into the matter in 1941 when Madagascar was under control of the Vichy French, from whom they could expect co-operation. The author's intention was to raise public awareness of the undesirability of this 'solution', concluding: 'The terrible risks involved in a mass settlement of white people in an isolated, backward, disease-ridden tropical wilderness are evident. They cannot be disregarded except by men who are completely devoid of all human feeling. The forced deportation of Jews *en masse* to the island of Madagascar must be resisted'.

157   **Japan's bid for Africa, the Madagascar campaign.**
Eric Rosenthal.   South Africa: Central News Agency, 1944. 172p. maps.

This rare book explains why British forces attacked Diego Suarez and subsequently, with some South African help, occupied the whole of Madagascar. After the Japanese fleet appeared in the Indian Ocean there was a danger that it might establish itself in the great harbour of Diego Suarez and disrupt the vital sea route round the Cape to the Middle East and India. It was thought unlikely that the French colonial government, which supported Vichy, would be able or willing to prevent this.

Africa South of the Sahara.
See item no. 7.

Histoire de la grande isle de Madagascar. (History of the great island of Madagascar.)
See item no. 31.

A paradox prooving that the inhabitants of Madagascar . . . are the happiest people in the world . . .
See item no. 32.

The voyages made by Sieur D.B. . . .
See item no. 33.

A voyage to Madagascar and the East Indies.
See item no. 34.

The last travels of Ida Pfeiffer.
See item no. 38.

Ethnology

General

158 **Les migrations intérieures à Madagascar, passée et présentes**. (The internal migrations in Madagascar, past and present.)
Hubert Deschamps. Paris: Berger-Levrault, 1959. 284p.

The author, one of the most distinguished authorities writing in French, was a District Officer in east and south-east Madagascar in the 1920s and 1930s. His book is a detailed academic study of the causes and consequences of internal migrations by the different ethnic groups, with statistics of the distribution of these groups in the various regions in the 1950s.

159 **Ethnographie de Madagascar.** (Ethnography of Madagascar.)
J. Faublée. Paris: Editions de France & d'Outre Mer, 1946. 168p. maps.

A basic work, written in collaboration with other scholars. It deals comprehensively but concisely with the techniques of hunting, fishing, agriculture and herding, handicrafts, housing and furniture, religion, etc. It is well-illustrated with photographs and many drawings of artefacts.

160 **Madagascar, island of the ancestors.**
John Mack. London: British Museum Publications, 1986. 96p. map. bibliog.

A complete and well-illustrated introduction to Malagasy culture produced in conjunction with the exhibition of the same name shown in London, New York and Antananarivo. The first part deals with history and the complex Malagasy belief system, it is particularly sound on the difficult concept of *vintana* (destiny). The second part, 'The living and the dead' provides the clearest and most readable summary available of the concept of the ancestors, funeral rites, tombs, cenotaphs, and funerary sculptures. An excellent bibliography leads easily to further studies.

161 **Les souverains de Madagascar: l'histoire royale et ses resurgence contemporaines.** (The sovereigns of Madagascar: royal history and its contemporary revival.)
Edited by Francoise Raison-Jourde.   Paris: Karthala, 1983. 476p. maps. bibliog. (Homme et Société).
This is not a comprehensive study of Malagasy kings and queens but a collection of academic essays by French, British and Malagasy scholars, covering various aspects of the institution of monarchy in different parts of Madagascar. The essays are grouped into four sections dealing respectively with symbolic structures and history; royal rituals; the exercise of power; and the impact of modern events, especially colonial rule, on the concept of royalty.

Ethnic groups

162 **Princes et paysans: les Tañala de l'Ikongo; un espace social du sud-est de Madagascar.** (Princes and peasants: the Tañala of the Ikongo; a social enclave in the south-east of Madagascar.)
Philippe Beaujard.   Paris: L'Harmattan, 1983. 671p.
The Tañala tribe form two groups, of which those of the Ikongo are by far the most independent. Ikongo is a mountain which provided a natural barrier against invasion, first by the Merina, then by the French. Written in an accessible style, this book is a very detailed sociological study of kinship, political organization and religious practices among these people. It is illustrated with many tables and photographs. The author has extended his study of the Tañala to their myths and folk tales: *Mythe et société à Madagascar* (Myth and society in Madagascar.) (Paris: L'Harmattan, 1991. 611p.). Here he relates twenty myths, with French and Malagasy texts, accompanied by an analysis and explanation of the legends.

163 **Vohimasina: village malgache; tradition et changement dans une société paysanne.** (Vohimasina: a Malagasy village; tradition and change in a peasant society.)
Bernard Chandon-Moët.   Paris: Nouvelle Editions Latines, 1972. 223p. maps. bibliog.
This is an interesting study of a village in the east, by the River Faraohy, north of Manakara. The aspects discussed include administration, agriculture, marriage and children, and the co-existence of the traditional power structure and officialdom.

164 **Les Zafimaniry: un groupe ethnique de Madagascar à la poursuite de la forêt; étude de géographie humaine.** (The Zafimaniry: an ethnic group of Madagascar in pursuit of the forest; a study in human geography.) Daniel Coulaud. Tananarive: Fanontam-Boky Malagasy, 1973. 385p. maps. bibliog.

The Zafimaniry inhabit a remaining fragment of forest in east-central Madagascar. They are noted for their distinctive culture which includes unique weaving methods and materials, and decorative wood carving. Since this book was written the Zafimaniry are under environmental and cultural threat as their forest continues to dwindle through slash-and-burn agriculture.

165 **Gender and social structure in Madagascar.** Richard Huntington. Bloomington, Indiana: Indiana University Press, 1988. 148p. maps. bibliog.

This is a study of the Bara people, written so that a layman can understand it. The author's aim is 'to present a general analysis of the broad outlines of Bara culture and society. . . through the study of gender categories'. He looks at Bara society in terms of maleness and femaleness, including marriage, incest, and feminine power.

166 **Madagascar: society and history.** Edited by Conrad P. Kottak, Jean-Aimé Rakotoarisoa, with Aidan Southall, Pierre Vérin. Durham, North Carolina: Carolina Academic Press, 1986. 443p. maps. bibliog.

This is a collection of papers prepared for the Burg Wartenstein Symposium no. 83 called 'Human adjustment in time and space in Madagascar'. The main themes of the symposium were Madagascar history, social organization and human ecological adaptation. About half of the papers are in French. Ethnic groups discussed in English are Anjoaty, Sakalava, Merina, Betsileo, Bara and Mahafaly.

167 **The past in the present: history, ecology and cultural variation in highland Madagascar.** Conrad P. Kottak, foreword by R. Rappaport. Ann Arbor, Michigan: University of Michigan Press, 1980. 339p. maps. bibliog.

Through this comparative study of three Betsileo communities, the author examines the main social changes which have affected this rice-growing, cattle-herding group since the 17th century. He uses a combination of historical and ecological perspectives with a concern with cultural adaptation to highlight the present state of the Betsileo. Although mainly for the specialist reader, there is a nice introductory section where a Betsileo man gives his own account of his culture.

168 **Customs and habits of the Merina tribe of Madagascar.** Kari Mason. Leicester, England: the Author, 1959. 39p.

A typewritten, mimeographed work written in straightforward language which provides an interesting insight into traditional practices of the Merina. The author was a member of the Académie malgache and was head of a girl's boarding school. She wanted to record the customs of the previous generation before they died out. Her account includes games, crafts, music, and such things of the past as cut money and

45

tangena (trial by poison). This work may be viewed at the Museum of Mankind, London.

169   **Freedom by a hair's breadth: Tsimihety in Madagascar.**
      Peter J. Wilson.   Ann Arbor, Michigan: Michigan University Press,
      1993. 179p. bibliog.

The Tsimihety are an ethnic group in the centre-north of Madagascar who have hitherto earned little attention from anthropologists. The author records how the Tsimihety achieved social and cultural autonomy largely by peaceful means. They slowly modified their social and cultural thinking and practices so as to make political, economic and cultural domination from the outside exceedingly difficult. The central theme of this work is the concept of freedom, and what it means to different cultures. This is an important book written in a lucid style that is accessible to the interested non-specialist.

Customs and beliefs

170   **Le Tsiny et le Tody dans la pensée malgache.** (Tsiny and Tody in
      Malagasy thinking.)
      Richard Andriamanjato.   Paris: Présence Africaine. 1957. 102p.

Tsiny means fault, usually a breach of the rules laid down by the ancestors. *Tody* has the basic meaning of 'arrival' after a difficult journey, but has the figurative meaning of the consquences of, or punishment for wrong actions. The author examines how these two concepts of fault and punishment govern the Malagasy thinking and help shape their reserved nature.

171   **From blessing to violence: history and ideology in the circumcism ritual**
      of the Merina of Madagascar.
      Maurice Bloch.   Cambridge, England; New York; Melbourne:
      Cambridge University Press, 1986. 214p. bibliog.

The author is one of the leading anthropologists writing about Madagascar. He begins with the politico-religious history of the Merina and their present-day social organization and religion, followed by details of their circumcision ritual and its symbolic significance.

172   **Placing the dead: tombs, ancestral villages, and kinship organisation in**
      Madagascar.
      Maurice Bloch.   New York: Seminar Press, 1971. 242p. bibliog.

This is a seminal work on ancestral customs, especially in relation to burial and family relationships in central Madagascar, which throws much light on present-day life and the background to the history of the Merina people.

173   **The political implications of religious experience.**
Maurice Bloch.   In: *Symbolic textures, studies in cultural meaning.*
Edited by Göran Aijmer.   Gothenburg, Sweden: University of
Gothenburg, 1987, p. 23-50.
The anthropologist here discusses the symbolism of domination in relation to Marxism:
'The power to influence and move people who are humiliated derives from the fact that
ideology makes domination desirable to inferiors by presenting it as part of a process
whereby the inferiors will ultimately become dominators'.

174   **La mort et les coutumes funéraires à Madagascar.** (Death and funereal
customs of Madagascar.)
Raymond Decary.   Paris: G. P. Maisonneuve et Laruse, 1962. 304p.
The author, founder of the Instititute of Scientific Research in Antananarivo, describes
the funerary practices of all the ethnic groups in Madagascar in considerable detail.
There are forty-two pages of illustrations.

175   **Un culte de possession à Madagascar: le tromba.** (A religion of spirit-
possession in Madagascar: the tromba.)
Jean-Marie Estrade.   Paris: Editions Anthropos, 1977. 391p. bibliog.
Tromba means spirit-possession. This important book discusses the phenomenon in
great detail, describing the origins of the *tromba* ritual, its power, and the place of
tromba in the culture of the various Malagasy ethnic groups.

176   **Malagasy customs and proverbs.**
Jean-Paul Koenig.   Sherbrooke, Canada: Editions Naaman, 1984. 52p.
The author was born and raised in Madagascar, learning about the customs and way of
life of the Malagasy from his Merina grandmother. This is not a scholarly book, but it
records traditions that have largely died out. On the subject of proverbs the author
writes: 'Among the Malagasy the use of proverbs is so widespread that it comes close
to being an irrepressible habit'.

177   **Le bain royal à Madagascar.** (The royal bath in Madagascar.)
Louis Molet.   Tananarive: Imprimerie Luthérienne, 1956. 236p.
In the Merina monarchy the new year was marked by the bathing of the sovereign
which symbolized the renewal of the monarchy. A similar custom was observed among
certain other ethnic groups. The author describes and analyses the significance of the
custom, its origins and history and also discusses tombs and funereal rites. This is an
important ethnological work.

178   **Ny atao no mi-verina. Ethnologie et proverbes malgaches.** (Malagasy
ethnology and proverbs.)
P. Gabriele Navone.   Fianarantsoa: Librairie Ambozontany, 1977.
268p. bibliog.
This is a scholarly study, in French, of Malagasy proverbs. Part 1 looks at the
structure, semantics, content, etc. of proverbs; and Part 2 studies the proverbs
themselves.

179 **Taboo: a study of Malagasy customs and beliefs.**
Jorgen Rund.   Oslo: Oslo University Press; London: George Allen &
Unwin. 1960. 324p.

Written in English by a Norwegian Lutheran missionary who worked for twenty years
in Madagascar, this is a detailed study of over 600 of the *fady* (taboos) which govern
nearly all aspects of life in Madagascar. It provides at the same time a valuable
ethnographic survey, covering the concept of *vintana* or destiny, tombs and burial
customs, marriage, birth and circumcision, animistic religion and plant and animal
taboos.

Histoire physique, naturelle et politique de Madagascar. (Physical, natural
history and political history of Madagascar.)
See item no. 1.

Madagascar and its people.
See item no. 2.

Madagascar: the great African island.
See item no. 3.

**Civilisation de l'est et du sud-est: archeologie, anthropologie sociale et art de
Madagascar.** (Civilization of the east and south-east: archaeology, social
anthropology, and art of Madagascar.)
See item no. 9.

La faune malgache: son rôle dans les croyances et les usages indigènes. (The
Malagasy fauna: its role in the beliefs and customs of the indigenous people.)
See item no. 89.

Madagascar in history: essays from the 1970s.
See item no. 106.

Collection des oeuvrages anciens concernant Madagascar. (A collection of
ancient works concerning Madagascar.)
See item no. 111.

The African element in Madagascar
See item no. 115.

Language

Origins

180 **The Bantu in Madagascar: the Malagasy race affinity.**
Emil Birkeli. *The Journal of African Society*, vol. 19 (1920),
p. 305-16.
A study of the Malagasy language, which is mainly an occidental branch of the Malayo-Polynesian group, with Arab, Swahili and older African (Bantu) elements.

181 **Langue, littérature et politique à Madagascar.** (Language, literature and politics in Madagascar.)
B. Domenichini-Ramiaramanana. Paris: Karthala, 1982. 664p.
A detailed study of how the early written Malagasy texts bring insights into the history of the island.

182 **Les manuscripts arabico-malgaches.** (The Arabic-Malagasy manuscripts.)
J. Faublée. *Bulletin Académie malgache* (1958) p. 983-89; (1962)
p. 1-3; (1965) p. 29.
These are three articles on the ancient *sorabe* manuscripts, bound into one volume in the Hardyman Collection (SOAS). Long before the missionaries from the London Missionary Society brought the written word to Madagascar in the first part of the 19th century there were sacred books in Arabic script, but in the Malagasy language. Villages in the east still have copies of these books, guarded by specially trained villagers who can also read the script.

Language study

183 **A concise introduction to the study of the Malagasy language as spoken in Imerina.**
W. E. Cousins.   Tananarive: London Missionary Society Press, 1894. 118p.

Missionaries from the London Missionary Society needed a thorough grasp of the Malagasy language, and used this book as their tutor. The author uses numerous examples and explanations to make the task as easy as possible.

184 **Les débuts de l'orthography malgache.** (The beginnings of Malagasy orthography.)
Otto Chr. Dahl.   Oslo: Universitetsforlaget, 1966. 52p. bibliog.

This study of Malagasy spelling was inspired by some letters and diaries written by British missionaries in 1823, and now in the archives of the London Missionary Society.

185 **Malagasy basics.**
Rasoanaivo Hanitrarivo.   London: F.M.S., 1992. 64p.

Designed primarily for tourists, this is the only readily-available modern language guide. With its accompanying cassette and clear presentation, it allows all visitors to have a basic understanding and use of the language. Available from the publisher (PO Box 337, London N4 1TW).

186 **Grammaire malgache.** (Malagasy grammar.)
Regis Rajemisa.   Fianarantsoa, Madagascar: Raolison, 1966. 174p.

Although written for the French speaker, this is the best introduction to the complicated grammatical structure of the Malagasy language.

187 **The causatives of Malagasy.**
Charles Randriamasimanana.   Honolulu, Hawaii: University of Hawaii Press, 1986. 682p. bibliog. (Oceanic Linguistic Special Publication no. 21.)

This is an immensely detailed specialist monograph analysing a wide range of syntactic phenomena and semantic distinctions in Malagasy grammar.

188 **Je parle couramment le malgache: I speak Malagasy fluently.**
Michel Razafindrabe, Xavier Ralahatra, Elisabeth Ravaoarimalala.
Fianarantsoa, Madagascar: L'Imprimer Sainte-Paul, 1984. 3 vols.

Instruction is given in both English and French, making this the best textbook for the serious student of the language.

189 **Malagasy without moans.**
   Elsie L. Stark.   Antananarivo: Trano Printy Loterana, 1969. 130p.
This is a practical and easy to follow first course on the Malagasy language for English-speaking students. Published in typewritten form and aimed at missionaries arriving in Madagascar to work for the London Missionary Society, it inevitably has a biblical bias. The author justifies this by pointing out that the Malagasy Bible has had the equivalent impact on the Malagasy language as the Authorised Bible has had on the English language.

Dictionaries and phrase books

190 **An elementary English-Malagasy dictionary.**
   Antananarivo: Trano Printy Loterana, 1969. 118p.
This contains 10,000 words most commonly used in modern English, but is only of value to the serious scholar since the Malagasy translation of most entries are five or six words long. A companion Malagasy-English dictionary entitled *Diksionera Malagasy-Englisy* was produced by the same publishers in 1973.

191 **English-Malagasy phrase book.**
   Antananarivo: Madprint. [n.d.]. 200p.
This is an adequate, recently published phrase book but it contains no phonetic pronunciation. A companion volume, *English-Malagasy vocabulary*, has been produced by the same publisher. This is a dictionary with some notes on grammar. Both volumes are available in Antananarivo.

192 **A dictionary of the Malagasy Language.**
   J. J. Freeman, D. Johns.   Tananarive: London Missionary Society
   Press, 1835. 2 vols.
Compliled from fifteen years' work, this is the most useful of all the dictionaries, although very few copies remain in circulation. Volume 1 by J. J. Freeman is English/Malagasy; and volume 2 by D. Johns is Malagasy/English.

193 **English-Malagasy vocabulary.**
   K. Paginton.   Antananarivo: Trano Printy Loterana, 1970. 192p.
An excellent vocabulary by the author of *A glance at Madagascar* (q.v.) which combines notes on the country with words and phrases of most use to the English-speaking visitor or resident. It includes short grammar notes, which allow the student to build his own sentences, and has a brief Malagasy-English supplement.

194 **A new Malagasy-English dictionary.**
James Richardson. Tananarive: London Missionary Society Press, 1885. Republished Farnborough, England: Gregg International, 1967. 2 vols.

Both volumes are Malagasy to English; this is a very detailed dictionary and of more value in the understanding of the Malagasy culture through the language than for practical use. For example there are words for the different ways of tying a 'lamba' or for the various markings on cattle. A helpful section on pronunciation and grammar adds to the importance of this book.

195 **Diksionary Englisy sy Malagasy.** (English-Malagasy dictionary.)
Joseph S. Sewell. Antananarivo: Friends' Foreign Mission Association, 1875. 380p.

This dictionary is clearly laid-out and comprehensive and would still be very useful for a student with an elementary understanding of the language.

Religion

General

196 **Les Jésuites à Madagascar au XIX siècle.** (The Jesuits in Madagascar in the 19th century.)
Père Adrien Boudou. Paris: Gabriel Beauchesne, 1940. 2 vols. maps. bibliog.
A detailed account of the work of the Jesuit missionaries in Madagascar. It gives the historical background from the first attempt to establish a mission in 1832, up to the early years of French colonial rule which greatly facilitated the expansion of Catholicism. This major book, written from a forty-year perspective, is remarkably objective and deals fairly with the activities of British and other missionaries.

197 **A man in shining armour: the story of the life of William Wilson.**
A. Crosfield. London: Headley, [1912?]. 278p.
William Wilson was the secretary of the Friends' Foreign Mission Association. A medical doctor, he worked in Madagascar up to the time of the French conquest. As the title suggests this is an uncritical biography but there is some interest in the descriptions of the Sakalava people, with whom he lived from 1884 to 1890.

198 **Friends in Madagascar, 1867-1967.**
London: Friends Service Council, 1967. 60p.
Published to mark the centenary of Quaker work in the island, this booklet is brief and factual, highlighting the major role that the Quakers played despite the far greater presence of the London Missionary Society.

Religion. General

199 **Madagascar and the Protestant impact. The work of the British missions 1818-1895.**
Bonar A. Gow. London: Longman & Dalhousie University Press, 1979. 266p. maps. bibliog. (Dalhousie African Studies Series).
In the 19th century Madagascar was the scene of one of the most successful Christian missions in the world, despite savage persecution under Queen Ranavalona I. The author's focus is on the period between 1861 and 1895, concentrating on the relationship between the missionaries and their flock of converts. He presents a somewhat one-sided view of the missionary character, accusing them of bigotry, racism and ignorance. While this is useful as a contrast to the missionaries' own accounts, the author is not always well-informed on the background which shaped their outlook, and there are numerous factual errors in the first part of the book covering the period from 1818 to 1861.

200 **Madagascar on the move.**
J. T. Hardyman. London: Livingstone Press, 1950. 234p.
This is a book about Madagascar, the church, and its history. It is aimed at helping new missionaries understand the changing conditions following the 1947 rebellion, when the spirit of nationalism was still evident.

201 **Une église des laïcs à Madagascar.** (A layman's church in Madagascar.)
Pietro Lupo. Paris: Editions du Centre National de la Recherche Scientifique, 1990. 432p.
Using Malagasy sources, the author reconstructs the year 1894-1895, which was significant in the history of the Catholic church in Madagascar because the local people took over the functions of the clergy. This is a complete religious, sociological and political portrait of the country at the dawn of the colonial period.

202 **Missionary to the Malagasy: the Madagascar diary of the Rev. Charles T. Price, 1875-1877.**
Edited by Arnold H. Price. New York; Bern; Frankfurt; Paris: Peter Lang, 1989. 261p. (American University Studies).
Charles Price was a missionary teacher who worked in Fianarantsoa, Ankafina and Ambositra. This is a fairly interesting journal which, being recently published, is more likely to be easily available than the London Missionary Society books issued at the turn of the century.

203 **La bible et le pouvoir à Madagascar au XIXe siècle.** (The Bible and power in Madagascar in the 19th century.)
Françoise Raison-Jourde. Paris: Karthala, 1991, 834p.
The author is a historian who taught in Madagascar from 1965 to 1973. Her book is subtitled: 'Invention of a Christian identity and construction of a state' and it reviews the influence of the British introduction of Christianity on the Malagasy culture. The missionaries not only brought the Bible, they brought writing and education. They also brought military advisers who trained the Merina army and enabled the Merina territory to be expanded. Two different worlds, traditional beliefs and an introduced culture, were in conflict. The result was the death of many martyrs and the creation of a military bourgeoisie and royal aristocracy. This is an important book which takes a

fresh look at Madagascar's 19th century history in the light of modern cultural understanding.

204 **Theologien-prêtre africain et developpement de la culture negro-africaine.** (The African theologian-priest and the development of the negro-African culture.)
Père Remi Ralibera. In: *Cahiers Présence Africaine*. Paris: Présence Africaine, 1964. p. 155-187.
A discussion on the relationship between Christianity and the vulnerable traditional belief system of Madagascar.

205 **Norwegian missions in African history.**
Edited by Jarle Simensen, Finn Fuglestad. Oslo: Norwegian University Press; Oxford: Oxford University Press, 1986. Vol. 2: Madagascar. 155p. maps.
This is a straightforward account of the missionaries and their work, with the aim of highlighting the political and social interaction between the missionaries and the local people. The British historian Stephen Ellis provided the background chapters on Madagascar. The first Norwegian (Lutheran) missionaries arrived in 1866 and there was rivalry soon developed between them and the long-established London Missionary Society. Between 1880 and 1890, when the French conquered Madagascar, the Norwegian influence was strongest in the south-west region and this is the most interesting section of the book.

206 **Histoire de Madagascar: ses habitants et ses missionnaires de Jesus.**
(History of Madagascar: her inhabitants and her Jesuit missionaries.)
Père de la Vaissiere. Paris: Librairie Victor Lecoffre. 1884. 2 vols.
Following chapters on earlier efforts by Catholic missionaries to gain a foothold in Madagascar, the bulk of the book deals in detail with the activities of Jesuit missionaries from 1844 to 1884, with lengthy excerpts from contemporary letters and diaries. The book contains much valuable information relating to the history of the period and especially the British Protestant/French Catholic rivalry. It is strongly biased against the British 'heretics' with the Rev. William Ellis of the London Missionary Society in particular being accused of improper behaviour in establishing Protestant ascendancy at the royal court.

London Missionary Society

207 **The people of the buried book.**
Iris Corbin. London: The Livingstone Press. [1935?]. 52p.
Written for Sunday school children, this work is of some value as a short history of the London Missionary Society in Madagascar, from the arrival of the first missionaries to the rebirth of Christianity under Queen Ranavalona II.

208 **The martyr church: a narrative of the introduction, progress, and triumph of Christianity in Madagascar.**
Rev. William Ellis. London: John Snow, 1869. 406p.
This is the standard work on the London Missionary Society period in Madagascar's history. Written with objectivity and humanity, it has some interesting observations on the pre-Christian morality of the Malagasy.

209 **A narrative of the persecution of the Christians in Madagascar, with details of the escape of the six Christian refugees now in England.**
Joseph John Freeman, David Johns. London: John Snow, 1840. 298p.
An interesting and pious account of the lives and deaths of the Malagasy Christian martyrs persecuted during the reign of Queen Ranavalona I. It is estimated that some 500 died. The authors, two of the pioneer missionaries of the 1820s, document the events of that period in some detail and provide some exciting narrative regarding the escape of the six Malagasy Christians to Mauritius and thence to England.

210 **The widowed missionary's journal.**
Keturah Jeffreys. Southampton, England: the Author, 1827. 216p.
Subtitled: 'Containing some account of Madagascar and also a narrative of the missionary career of the Rev. J. Jeffreys who died on a passage from Madagascar to the Isle of France, July 4 1825'. This period was very early in the London Missionary Society members' activities in Madagascar and this unpretentious and nicely-written book provides good insights into the life and personages of those times from a woman's viewpoint. The author printed the book to raise money to support her four children.

211 **Thirty years in Madagascar.**
Rev. T. T. Matthews. London: The Religious Tract Society, 1904. 384p. map.
The author worked for the London Missionary Society in central Madagascar, and apart from early chapters of history, taken from William Ellis, the emphasis is on missionary work, with the Malagasy people observed from a Christian standpoint.

212 **Thomas Rowlands of Madagascar.**
Edward Rowlands, Emrys Rowlands. London: The Livingstone Press, [192–?]. 111p.
A pious and loyal account of the work of a Welsh missionary in the Betsileo town of Ambohimandroso. The style is uninspiring, but it provides an interesting insight into Madagascar during the reign of Queen Ranavalona II, and the effect of the French invasion and subsequent colonization.

213 **Fifty years in Madagascar.**
Rev. James Sibree. London: Allen & Unwin, 1924. 360p. map.
This is the last major work by Sibree and is mainly a summary of his missionary activities. As always, it is laced with fascinating observations of the Malagasy and their customs, and of his varied experiences in the country, starting as a young architect responsible for building the Martyr Memorial Churches and later as principal of the

London Missionary Society College in Antananarivo for thirty years. The book is well-illustrated with photographs.

214 **Ten years' review of mission work in Madagascar: 1870-1880.**
Tananarive: The London Missionary Society, 1880. 320p.
A statistical review of the missionary work during this period, mainly of use to scholars and researchers. There are some interesting descriptions of areas outside Imerina.

215 **Madagascar: its missionaries and martyrs.**
William Townsend. London: S. W. Partridge, [n.d.]. 160p.
A volume aimed at young people and Sunday schools and based on the writings of William Ellis (q.v.). This is a very pious book, but quite a readable potted history of the subject.

Africa South of the Sahara.
See item no. 7.

Among the Malagasy: an unconventional record of missionary experience.
See item no. 35.

Twelve months in Madagascar.
See item no. 37.

From Fianarantsoa to Ikongo.
See item no. 39.

History of Madagascar.
See item no 130.

Social Conditions

General

216 **Les poubelles de la survie: la décharge municipale de Tananarive.** (The dustbins of survival: the municipal rubbish dump of Tananarive.)
Martine Comacho. Paris: L'Harmattan, 1986. 208p.

The unprepossessing title of this work conceals some fascinating material. This is not a study of waste disposal but of the people who live off the city rubbish dump. In the mid-1980s they numbered 300 or so. The book is a sociological study of the very poor, much enlivened by character studies of some of the people for whom Kianja, the dump, is their only means for survival.

217 **Woman in Madagascar: her position and influence, especially in Christian effort.**
James Sibree. In: *Fifty years in Madagascar*. London: Allen & Unwin, 1924, p. 255-64.

In this chapter Sibree takes a perceptive look at the role of women in Madagascar at the end of the 19th century and early 20th century. He notes that they occupy a higher social place than in African countries, probably because of the Merina queens who ruled the country for much of the 19th century. Tribal chiefs were often women. In addition to examining their role in society, he looks at their traditional activities in agriculture and crafts. On the same subject is *La femme malgache avant la colonisation* (The Malagasy woman before colonization) selected by Suzy Andrée Ramamonjisoa, Georgelle Razafindrabe (Tananarive: Edition Direction de la Recherche Scientifique et Technique, 1976. 268p.). This is a compilation of texts on the subject of women and their position in traditional Malagasy society.

218 **Des femmes malgaches: reflets d'aujourd'hui.** (Malagasy women: reflections of today.)
Edited by the Soroptimist International Club d'Antananarivo.
Antananarivo: Editions Tsipika. [198–?]. 94p.

Provides portraits of women in Tulear and Antananarivo, with case studies which describe the place of women in their community. This book is available in Antananarivo.

Colonialism

219 **A green estate: restoring independence in Madagascar.**
Gillian Feeley-Harnik. Washington, DC: Smithsonian Institute, 1991. 648p. bibliog.

Through a study of society (work, kings, gender, etc.) and the colonial economic and political structure, the author promotes an understanding of how the reburial of a king, who died in colonial times, symbolizes rights reasserted over land and cultural heritage.

220 **Prospero and Caliban: the psychology of colonization.**
O. Mannoni, translated from French by Pamela Powesland. London: Methuen, 1956. 218p. bibliog.

The author uses his experiences in colonial Madagascar to focus on the psychological effects of colonization on the colonizer and colonized. He points out how the Malagasy, emerging from the security of tribal life, were particularly vulnerable to feelings of dependence and how well this fitted the colonists' desire for authority in an unfamiliar land. This is an important book, although the personal nature of the author's observations and conclusions will inevitably jar with some readers. In the context of its time, when the countries of Africa and the Indian Ocean were moving towards independence, some valuable insights emerge which have relevence to the changing political scene in the 1990s.

Health

221 **Patients, healers and doctors in a polyethnic society.**
Jean Benoist. *African Environment*, vol. 1, no. 4 (1975), p. 40-64.

Most of this study centres round the French island of Réunion, but the author uses the example of traditional healers in Madagascar to illustrate 'last resort' medicine. He compares the use of traditional Malagasy medicine with that used by a small-scale European farmer.

222 **The experience of Madagascar in the field of industrial medicine.**
Pierre Delaunay. *Inter-African Labour Institute Bulletin*, vol. 9, no. 3
(Aug. 1962), p. 21-36.

This presents a study of health and safety at work. The first part is about the rules and
regulations of the work place, followed by the organization and implementation of
these rules. The third part covers the limitations of these policies in the context of the
Third World. On p. 5-20 of the same issue the article is printed in French, entitled
'L'experience de Madagascar en matière de médecine d'entreprise'.

Africa South of the Sahara.
See item no. 7.

Ratsiraka: socialisme et misère à Madagascar.
(Ratsiraka: socialism and poverty in Madagascar.)
See item no. 226.

**La logique des agricultures de transition. L'exemple des sociétés paysannes
malgaches.** (The logic of transitional agricultures. The example of Malagasy
peasant societies.)
See item no. 257.

Politics

223 **Madagascar depuis 1972: la marche d'une révolution.** (Madagascar
since 1972: the progress of a revolution.)
Robert Archer.   Paris: L'Harmattan, 1976. 210p.
This was translated into French from the work of a British postgraduate history student
who carried out research on Madagascar in the early 1970s. It was written with the aid
of Malagasy students and university teachers who took an active part in the 'revolution'
which led to the downfall of the first Malagasy Republic in 1972. This may account for
the somewhat biased attitude to the outgoing regime and the tendency to a Marxist
analysis of the political and social structure. Nevertheless, this is an illuminating study
of the causes of the 'revolution' and of the subsequent struggle for power from which
Ratsiraka emerged in 1975 as a president committed to a Socialist revolution. There is
a useful appendix giving details of the successive governments from 1972 to 1976 and
the main political parties.

224 **Contribution à l'histoire de la nation malgache.** (A contribution to the
history of the Malagasy nation.)
Pierre Boiteau.   Paris: Editions Sociales, 1958. 432p.
The author was a committed communist who was sent out to Madagascar in the 1930s
by the Communist Party of France to set up unions and help guide the nationalist
movement; he remained active there until independence. This is history from an anti-
imperialist standpoint and as such provides a useful contrast to most accounts of this
period. It is particularly helpful on the rise of nationalism in Madagascar.

225 **Madagascar: politics, economics and society.**
Maureen Covell.   London; New York: Frances Pinter, 1987. 187p.
(Marxist Regime Series).
This is one of the best books on post-colonial politics and economics; it puts the
Malagasy experience of Marxism in its historical and sociological context. The
Malagasy people have tried to integrate their traditions with Marxism, introduced in
1975 under President Ratsiraka. This is an academic book with many tables.

226 **Ratsiraka: socialisme et misère à Madagascar.** (Ratsiraka: socialism and poverty in Madagascar.)
Ferdinand Déléris. Paris: L'Harmattan, 1986. 140p.

As the title indicates, this is not an unbiased account. The author was a colonial official who served in Madagascar from 1959 to 1969 as Director of Economic Affairs and then as adviser to the Foreign Minister. While not uncritical of certain aspects of the colonial regime and the neo-colonial aspects of the post-independence decade, he defends the economic achievements of that period. Through some telling statistics he demonstrates that Ratsiraka's socialism was largely responsible for the economic collapse of the early 1980s. He also denounces the political repression and denial of human rights under the 'revolutionary socialist' regime of Ratsiraka.

227 **Le livre vert de l'espérance malgache.** (The green book of Malagasy hope.)
Lucile R. Ramanandraibe. Paris: L'Harmattan. 1987. 136p.

A counter blast to Ratsiraka's 'Red book' by a former diplomat who was a co-founder of an opposition movement in exile: Union des Opposants malgaches à l'Exterieur (UOME) in Paris in 1987. In four chapters dealing with democracy, economic problems, social problems and foreign policy, it denounces the failure of revolutionary socialism and sets out democratic, non-socialist alternatives for Madagascar.

228 **Le parti communiste de la region de Madagascar. 1930-1939.** (The Communist Party in the Madagascar region. 1930-1939.)
Sololo Randrianja. Antananarivo: Foi et Justice, 1989. 179p.

A valuable account of the Malagasy branch of the French Communist Party which was set up under the Popular Front Government in 1936 but disintegrated two years later. As the first modern political party in Madagascar it attracted many nationalists, although few of them were Marxists. The author places the Communist Party in the context of the nationalist movement between 1915 and 1947, and demonstrates that many former members of the Communist Party were actively involved in the rebellion of 1947.

Africa South of the Sahara.
See item no. 7.

Notre unité et l'époque colonial. (Our unity and the colonial period.)
See item no. 136.

Des femmes malgaches: reflets d'aujourd'hui. (Malagasy women: reflections of today.)
See item no. 218.

A green estate: restoring independence in Madagascar.
See item no. 219.

Mauritius, Madagascar, Seychelles: Country Report.
See item no. 246.

Legal System

229 **Sources et tendances du droit moderne à Madagascar.**
(Sources and tendencies of modern law in Madagascar.)
Louis Molet. *Canadian Journal of African Studies*, vol 1, no. 2
(Nov. 1967), p. 123-34.
The sources of Malagasy law lie in the ancient writings preserved in sacred manuscripts written in arabic script and known as *sorabe*, and preserved by certain ethnic groups in the south and south-east; and in the local oral traditions. Later the Europeans, British and French, introduced their own laws.

230 **Le droit de la famille à Madagascar.** (Family rights in Madagascar.)
H. Raharijaona. In: *Droit de la famille en Afrique et à Madagascar.*
Edited by M'Baye. France: G. P. Maisonneuve et Larose, 1968.
A report from the International Association of Legal Science, concerning Malagasy law and written by the President of the Court of Appeal. Among matters discussed are the modern changes in the family, children's rights, and the legal protection of women.

231 **Traité de droit civil malgache: les lois et coutumes Hovas.** (Treaty of
Malagasy civil law: the Hova laws and customs.)
E-P. Thébault. Tananarive: R. de Comarmond; Paris: Jouve, 1953.
3 vols.
The author, who was vice-president of the Court of Appeal in Madagascar, wrote this work during the French colonial period, detailing the pre-colonial law of the Hova.

232 **Traité de droit civil malgache moderne.** (Treaty of modern Malagasy civil law.)
E-P. Thébault.   Tananarive: Librairie de Madagascar, 1964. 230p. (Les Codes Bleu malgaches).

This is a detailed and complete textbook written shortly after independence. In the same series is *La justice administrative à Madagascar* (Administrative justice of Madagascar) by J-P. Masseron, (1963); and *Précis de droit du travail à Madagascar* (Precis of occupational law in Madagascar) by P. Palazzo, (1964).

Administration and
Local Government

233 **Fokonolona et collectivités rural en Imerina.** (The fokonolona and rural
communities in Imerina.)
Georges Condominas. Paris: Berger-Levrault, 1960.
Fokonolona, also spelled Fokon'olona, means 'people's assembly'. The concept was
introduced by King Andrianampoinimerina in the late 18th century, when these
bodies, essentially councils of village elders, were given responsibilities at village level
for law and order, the settlement of petty disputes, the organization of unpaid labour
and the collection of taxes. Their importance declined over the years owing to the
autocratic, centralizing nature of both the Merina monarchy and French colonial rule.
Condominas, a leading French ethnologist, wrote this authoritative work shortly after
the colonial administration had tried to revive the fokonolona in the form of
'collectivités autochtones rurales' with the aim of promoting grass-roots economic
development. Another book on this subject published ten years earlier, so with more
of a historical perspective, is *Le fokon'olona à Madagascar* (The fokon'olona in
Madagascar) by Francis Arbousset (Paris: Editions Domat Montchrestien, 1950.
306p.).

234 **L'administration publique à Madagascar.** (Public administration in
Madagascar.)
Michel Massiot. Paris: Librairie Général de Droit et de Jurisprudence.
[n.d.] 446p.
The translation of the subtitle is: 'Evolution of the administrative territorial
organization of Madagascar from 1896', and this is an exhaustive study of the subject.
The first French Governor-General, Gallieni, established an administrative framework
of twenty provinces, subdivided into districts and cantons, retaining the hierarchy of
Malagasy officials, headed by Governors and Deputy Governors, but subordinated to
French 'chefs de province' and 'chefs de district'. Subsequent Governors altered the
numbers of provinces and districts before the present framework, based on six
provinces, was established just before independence. However, the aim of decentraliza-
tion, to make the government more reponsive to the needs of the people, was usually
frustrated by the authoritarian, centralizing tradition of French colonial administration.

Administration and Local Government

The same author has written *L'organisation politique, administrative, financière et judiciaire de la République malgache.* (The political, administrative, financial and judiciary organization of the Malagasy Republic) (Antananarivo: Editions Librairie de Madagascar, 1970).

Foreign Relations

235 **Cent années de rivalité coloniale: France et Angleterre – l'affaire de Madagascar.** (A hundred years of colonial rivalry: France and England – the Madagascar affair.)
Jean Darcy. Paris: Librairie Académique. 1908. 162p.
The Franco-British colonial rivalry in Madagascar was not an equal contest at the government level. The British government had no ambitions to colonize Madagascar whereas the French had nurtured a claim to sovereignty since the 17th century. The rivalry over religion was much more serious between the very successful British missionaries, principally from the London Missionary Society, and the Jesuits whose influence greatly strengthened after the French occupation in 1895. This account, like most other French accounts of the period, is essentially an attempt to justify the French claims to sovereignty.

236 **The drama of Madagascar.**
Sonia Howe. London: Methuen, 1938. 360p.
The author examines Madagascar from the standpoint of foreign relations, specifically the relationship between Britain and France, the two competing colonial powers. Because Madagascar lay on the route to India from the Cape of Good Hope it was of vital importance to the mariners of all nations since ships could reprovision there. The book contains much original material from the court minutes of the East India Company, and the Colonial Office in Paris.

237 **La nouvelle diplomatie malgache.** (The new Malagasy diplomacy.)
Philippe Leymare. *Le Mois en Afrique*, no. 97 (1974), p. 29-40.
This is an interview with the future President D. Ratsiraka, who at the time was foreign misinster, reaffirming the financial and political independence of Madagascar from France, and a policy of non-alignment.

238 **The Malagasy and the Europeans: Madagascar's foreign relations 1861-1895.**
Phares Mutibwa. London: Longman, 1974. 412p. (Ibadan History Series).

This work is based on a doctoral thesis, by a Ugandan, on the relations between Madagascar, France and England in the 35 years leading up to its becoming a French protectorate. The book is less reliable in the chapters that fall outside the author's specialist area.

239 **Les relations extérieures de Madagascar de 1960 à 1972.** (Foreign relations of Madagascar from 1960 to 1972.)
Césaire Rabenoro. Paris: L'Harmattan, 1986. 356p.

The author, who is president of the Académie malgache, served as ambassador in London and State Secretary for Foreign Affairs in the First Republic (1960-72), and as Minister for Foreign Affairs in the transitional government of 1991-93. The book, based on a doctoral thesis, is a comprehensive and thorough review of the underlying principles and detailed practice of Madagascar's foreign relations under the Tsiranana government. It also describes the geographical, historical, and social background together with the economic circumstances and internal politics of the country which helped to shape foreign policy.

240 **Malgaches et Américains: relations commerciales et diplomatique au XIXeme siècle.** (Malagasy and Americans: commercial and diplomatic relations in the 19th century.)
G. Michael Razi. [privately printed], 1985. 175p.

The author was the Information Officer in the US Embassy in Antananarivo in the 1970s. He describes all aspects of the relationship between Madagascar and America, including whaling.

241 **French policy towards the Chinese in Madagascar.**
Leon M. S. Slawecki. Hamden, Connecticut: Shoe String Press, 1971. 265p. 4 maps, bibliog.

In the 1970s the Chinese community in Madagascar was the largest in Africa (10,000). The French, who had brought in Chinese labourers, and the subsequent Malagasy governments were suspicious of these Chinese residents, fearing Communist subversion, but government policies were always cautious because of the economic power of the Chinese. For his thesis for Yale University the author made use of French and Malagasy archive material as well as interviews and questionnaires among the Chinese in Madagascar.

Africa South of the Sahara.
See item no. 7.

Madagascar and France.
See item no. 147.

Economy

242 The Africa Review: the Economic and Business Report.
Saffron Walden, England: Walden Publishing, 1976- . annual.
The section on Madagascar contains about four pages of political review and a business guide, written by Mervyn Brown.

243 Economic development cycles in Madagascar, 1950-89.
Rajaona Andriamananjara.   In: *Economic planning and performance in Indian Ocean Island states*. Edited by R. T. Appleyard and R. N. Ghosh.   Canberra: Australian National University, 1990. p. 1-19.
This is a review of the performance of Madagascar's economy from the ten years leading up to independence to the last years of the Ratsiraka government, assessing the relevance and impact of various economic policies.

244 Madagascar: its capabilities and resources.
Captain E. W. Dawson.   London: George Philip & Sons, 1895. 83p. maps.
After looking carefully into the natural resources of Madagascar, the author came to the conclusion that 'Madagascar only requires the advent of railways and roads to make it one of the most prosperous commercial countries of the world'. The book contains some work projects accompanied with an evaluation of costs, for example for building railway stations and rest houses at Antananarivo, Majunga, and Tamatave. Some of these project ideas are still valid. The book provides an interesting comparison with the gloomy economic outlook of the present day.

245 **Structural disequilibria and adjustment programmes in Madagascar.**
Gilles Duruflé. In: *Structural adjustment in Africa*. Edited by Bonnie
K. Campbell, John Loxley. Basingstoke, England: Macmillan, 1989,
p. 169-201. (Macmillan International Political Economy Series).

Economic and financial crisis began in Madagascar in the early 1980s, due to a number
of factors, which are discussed. In 1986 the World Bank proposed a scenario for
resolving the crisis, based on better agricultural price incentives and a greater role
given to market forces. However, there was widespread opposition to the adjustment
policies, which led to the perpetuation of the dysfunctioning of markets and the
disruption of efforts directed to encourage a renewal of production and exports.

246 **Mauritius, Madagascar, Seychelles: Country Report.**
Economist Intelligence Unit. London: Economist Intelligence Unit,
1993- . quarterly.

This was previously published as *Madagascar, Mauritius, Seychelles, Comoros: Country
Report*. It provides an analysis of economic and political trends in two parts: outlook
(for the next eighteen months) and review (for the past three months). The
Madagascar section comprises about ten pages which cover the political scene, the
economy, finance, agriculture and fishing, industry and energy, communications and
tourism, and foreign trade. These include statistics and regional comparisons. The
Economist Intelligence Unit also publishes *Madagascar: Country Profile*, which
appears annually and gives more background information. A bi-annual report on the
economy and politics of the country is *Madagascar: Abecor Country Report*,
distributed by Barclays Bank.

247 **Madagascar.**
Nigel Heseltine. London: Pall Mall, 1971. 334p. maps. bibliog.
(Library of African Affairs).

The author was economic adviser to the first president of independent Madagascar,
Philibert Tsiranana. He is good on history, but the strength of the book is its excellent
chapters on economics, statistics and development prospects. The latter includes
details of the first Five Year Plan, from 1964 to 1969. The bibliography is very
thorough.

248 **L'évolution économique de Madagascar de la première à la seconde
république.** (The evolution of the economy in Madagascar from the first
to the second republic.)
P. Hugon. *Le Mois en Afrique*, no. 143 (1977), p. 26-57.

On independence in 1960 Madagascar adopted the capitalist system, joining the Franc
Zone under which France continued to enjoy a privileged economic position in return
for supporting the Malagasy franc. Following the collapse of the pro-French
government in 1972, Madagascar asserted its economic independence and left the
Franc Zone. After a period of turmoil, the Second Republic, based on 'revolutionary
socialism', was established in 1975. This is a study of the early days of the new socialist
policy, including the nationalizations and centralized economic control which were to
contribute largely to the collapse of the economy in the early 1980s.

249 **Le situation economique.** (The economic situation.)
Ministère des Finances et du Plan. Antananarivo: Institut National de
la Statistique et de la Recherche Economique. annual.

This report gives statistics on all aspects of the economy: industrial production,
transport, export, prices and capital investment. Copies from the 1970s and 80s are
available for view in the Hardyman Collection.

250 **Malawi and Madagascar.**
Frederic L. Pryor. New York: Oxford University Press, 1991. 484p.
(The Political Economy of Poverty, Equity and Growth).

This series, sponsored by the World Bank, makes comparative studies of economic
systems. Here the author takes two very different but equally poor countries, and
provides a comparison of their economic systems and long-term economic policies.
Malawi chose a market economy whilst Madagascar, after 1975, was committed to a
planned economy. Neither country has been successful in alleviating poverty. The
book answers three critical questions: Why have these countries chosen such different
economic institutions and strategies of development? What policies have the
governments implemented to realize their different goals? How have such policies
affected economic growth and the distribution of income?

251 **Madagascar: une économie en phase d'ajustment.** (Madagascar: an
economy in a period of adjustment.)
Olivier Ramahatra. Paris: L'Harmattan, 1989. 288p.

Written by a former economic adviser to the President, this book analyses the
proposals of the international monetary agencies to revive Madagascar's economy.
Supported by a large amount of statistical information he aims to show the limitations
of these financial measures, and investigates the best means to steer the country
through its inevitable period of adjustment.

252 **Le développement en quête d'acteurs-entreprises – le cas de la province
de Tananarive.** (Development in quest of self-help projects – the case
of Antananarivo province.)
Roland Ramahatra. Mauritius: Editions de l'Ocean Indien, 1990,
194p.

This book was sponsored by UNICEF and written by the brother of Olivier Ramahatra
(q.v.). It is an analysis of projects run by non-government organizations involving the
distribution of medicine, reforestation programmes and road maintenance. The author
emphasizes the joint efforts made by the local people and the various organizations.
The example of a small village called Ambohitrimanjaka, near Antananarivo, is used
to show what can be achieved when local interests are considered. The villagers' needs,
their culture, and above all their abilities, were all taken into account. This is a
readable, optimistic book which offers help and encouragement for those involved with
aid projects in Madagascar.

Africa South of the Sahara.
See item no. 7.

Economy

Madagascar: étude géographique et économique.
See item no. 18.

Mineral resources of the Malagasy Republic.
See item no. 23.

Bulletin d'Information et de Statistiques. (Bulletin of Information and Statistics.)
See item no. 268.

Trade and Industry

253 **Le régime des mines d'or à Madagascar.** (The organization of gold
     mines in Madagascar.)
     R. Augier. Paris: Ollier-Henry. 1920, 120p.
The first part of this thesis covers the geographical locations of the gold mines, then the
author makes a comparative study of French and South African legislation concerning
gold mines. The third section describes the local rules and the different techniques of
gold extraction.

254 **Report on the role of industry and crafts in the urban growth of black
     Africa and Madagascar.**
     R. J. Harrison. *La Croissance Urbaine en Afrique Noire et
     Madagascar*, no. 539 (Sep.-Oct. 1970), p. 111-16.
The author gives a definition of artistic crafts and their utilitarian counterparts and
trade craftsmen. He feels that since the artistic crafts are dying out for a variety of
reasons, the mass production of utilitarian crafts should be encouraged.

Africa South of the Sahara.
See item no. 7.

Through western Madagascar in quest of the golden bean.
See item no. 36.

**Madagascar, an historical and descriptive account of the island and its former
dependencies.**
See item no. 135.

Mauritius, Madagascar, Seychelles: Country Report.
See item no. 246.

Agriculture

General

255 Le question agraire à Madagascar: administration et paysannat de 1895 à nos jours. (The agrarian question in Madagascar: administration and the peasantry from 1895 to our times.)
Dominique Desjeux.   Paris: L'Harmattan. 1979. 195p.
The author approaches the political and sociological aspects of agriculture, rice culture in particular, by comparing the Malagasy peasant farmer with his counterpart in mainland Africa. He points out that Madagascar is the only country in the African world to have achieved a system of land management, between 1977 and 1978, not by the arbitrary nomination of officials, but through election. The author taught sociology at the Agricultural School (l'école d'agronomie) in Madagascar.

256 Sainte-Marie de Madagascar: insularité et économie du girofle. (Sainte-Marie of Madagascar: insularity and economy of cloves.)
Elyane-Tiana Rahonintsoa.   Antananarivo. Université de Madagascar, 1978. approx 150p. 4 maps.
Despite the spices cloves and vanilla being a major part of the agriculture of Madagascar there are few books on the subject. This exhaustive study of Sainte-Marie is divided into two parts. Half its pages are an analysis of the clove industry, with details on how the spice is grown and marketed. One of the maps shows the distribution of the clove plantations. The first part of this mimeographed university thesis examines other aspects of the island: history, including the period when it served as a prison island; fishing and subsistence agriculture; and the beginnings of a tourist industry.

257 **La logique des agricultures de transition. L'exemple des sociétés
paysannes malgaches.** (The logic of transitional agricultures. The
example of Malagasy peasant societies.)
Jean-Claude Rouveyrau.   Antananarivo: Maisonneuve et Larose, with
the University of Antananarivo, 1972. 276p. bibliog.
A very detailed book which examines all aspects of subsistance agriculture, using
Madagascar as an example. The author recognizes the constraints that are imposed on
peasant farmers by their traditions, their conservatism, and their respect for higher
members of the social hierarchy such as priests, community chiefs and politicians. In
addition they are manipulated by the outsiders and foreigners who are in control of the
development programmes, and who have an insufficient understanding of local customs
and taboos. Tradition and progress thus become antagonistic forces.

Cattle

258 **Cattle, economics and development.**
R. Crotty.   Slough, England: Commonwealth Agricultural Bureau,
1980. 253p.
Although not specific to Madagascar, this analysis of the contribution of cattle to the
economic welfare of developing countries, is of great interest to professionals working
with or studying the zebu cattle of Madagascar.

259 **La boeuf dans la vie malgache.** (Cattle in the Malagasy life.)
Raymond Delval.   Paris: the Author, 1986. 151p.
Zebu cattle are central to the lives of the rural Malagasy, being important, through
sacrifice, as a link with the ancestors, and an outward indication of wealth, as well as a
source of food. This is a marvellously complete book on every aspect: symbolic and
social significance; the importance of cattle to the economic and political life; cattle-
rustling; legends and proverbs; and language, such as the Malagasy names for colours
and markings. Nothing has been omitted and there are plenty of photographs and
diagrams. This book may be viewed in the Hardyman Collection (SOAS).

Rice

260 **Le riz et la riziculture à Madagascar.** (Rice and rice culture in
Madagascar.)
Yoshia Abé.   Paris: Editions du Centre National de la Recherche
Scientific, 1984. 232p. bibliog.
This is a learned study of rice cultivation in Imerina. It is divided into four sections:
rice and rice culture; ecological conditions; cultural techniques of *tavy* (burning); and
'hill' rice culture. Included are practical methods of subsistence rice growing in the

highlands, the historical development of rice growers during the Merina monarchy, and the evolution of techniques in rice cultivation in Imerina.

261 **Riziculture and the founding of the monarchy in Imerina.**
G. M. Berg. *The Journal of African History*, vol 22, no. 3 (1981), p. 289-308.

The cultivation of paddy rice spread from the east coast of Madagascar to Imerina and the southern plateau. In Imerina it enhanced the value of co-operative labour among isolated communities where the control of water meant the control of society, thus hastening the evolution of a rigid social hierarchy.

262 **Hommes et paysages du riz a Madagascar.** (Men and rice landscapes in Madagascar.)
Françoise le Bourdiec. Antananarivo: Foiben-Taosarin-Tanin'i Madagascar, 1978. 648p.

The Malagasy are the largest consumers of rice in the world, and have an almost mystical attachment to it, as is shown in many of their proverbs and taboos. The Betsileo are the masters of rice cultivation, but it is grown throughout the island, either in irrigated paddies or as 'hill rice' watered by the rain. This scholarly book, subtitled 'a study in human geography', covers the complex relationship between man and rice in Madagascar.

263 **Madagascar: perspectives from the Malay world.**
Edited by Yoshikazu Takaya. Kyoto, Japan: Kyoto University, Center for Southeast Asian Studies, 1988. 262p. maps.

This is the interim report of the project 'Studies on traditional rice culture in Madagascar in relation to the "Malay" agriculture'. It discusses the historical aspects of rice cultivation in both Madagascar and south-east Asia, drawing parallels between present-day methods of cultivation in the two societies. It includes a description of the Tsimihety culture and the importance of rice to this ethnic group.

Africa South of the Sahara.
See item no. 7.

Mauritius, Madagascar, Seychelles: Country Report.
See item no. 246.

Transport and Communications

264 Labour and the transport problem in imperial Madagascar, 1810-1895.
Gwyn Campbell. *The Journal of African History*, vol 21, no. 3 (1980),
p. 341-56.

In Madagascar the use of human labour for the transport of goods and travellers was
necessary in the 19th century because of the deliberate absence of roads, in order to
discourage foreign invaders; it became self-perpetuating because the use of forced
labour and slaves made the investment in alternative transport arrangements
unattractive. An indigenous 'proto-trade union' of the *maromita* (porters) was created
although it had no power. When the French colonial government instituted a modern
road and rail transport network from 1895, the imperial porterage system disintegrated.

265 Les chemins de fer et tramways des colonies. (Railways and tramways in
the colonies.)
Charles Rotté. Paris: Emile Larose, Libraire-editeur, 1910. 355p.

Although Madagascar does not have an extensive network of railways, the French
colonial government recognized the necessity of railways in a country with virtually no
roads. When this book was published the most important line, 375 kilometres long,
was in the process of being laid, linking the main port, Tamatave, with the capital.
Three other shorter lines followed. The book covers all the French colonies, including
Madagascar, and is divided into three parts. The first considers the practicalities of
installing railways in the colonies, the measures needed for their installation and the
administrative and financial organization. The second part is an analysis of the colonies
which already had railways, looking at the development of the existing rail network or
of additional railways. The third part is a study of the countries which did not have
railways and the consequences. The analysis of the economic aspects of the
development of communication is still valid. In the early part of the century the
benefits would be to the cities, but in modern times they aid the entire country.

266 **Perspective de développement des télécommunications par satellites en Afrique et à Madagascar.** (A perspective on the development of telecommunications by satellite in Africa and Madagascar.)
A. Vivet. *Coopération et développement*, no. 18 (1967), p. 27-36.

Details of the technology of satellite telecommunications, which in Madagascar includes satellite television, are followed by a list of the main projects and works in progress. In conclusion the author analyses the space technology required in Africa and Madagascar.

Africa South of the Sahara.
See item no. 7.

Madagascar, an historical and descriptive account of the island and its former dependencies
See item no. 135.

Mauritius, Madagascar, Seychelles: Country Report.
See item no. 246.

Statistics

267 **La démographie quantitative. Concepts et méthodes d'analyse: establissment d'enseignement supérieur de droit, d'economie, de gestion et de sociologie.** (Quantitative demography. Concepts and methods of analysis: the establishment of higher education in law, economics, management and sociology.)
Bruno Disaine Andriamboahangy.   Antananarivo: University of Madagascar, [n.d.] 244p.
A detailed and complete manual for teaching and interpreting population statistics.

268 **Bulletin d'Information et de Statistiques.** (Bulletin of Information and Statistics.)
Banque Centrale de Madagascar.   Antananarivo: Banque Centrale de Madagascar, new series 1990- . quarterly.
A statistical review of the Madagascar economy. This was previously published monthly as *Bulletin mensuel de statistiques.*

269 **Publications de l'Institut de la Statistique et de la Recherche Economique.** (Publications of the Institute of Statistics and Economic Research.)
Institut de la Statistique.   Antananarivo: Direction Général de la Banque de Données de l'État. annual.
An annual publication containing statistical information on the economy, population, and external commerce in Madagascar. The following separate reports are also available: *Statistiques du commerce exterior* (statistics for overseas business); *Situation*

économique (Economic situation); *Recensement industriel* (Industrial census). The published information is five or six years in arrears.

Africa South of the Sahara.
See item no. 7.

Education

270 **L'organisation de l'enseignement à Madagascar 1896-1905.** (The organization of education in Madagascar 1896-1905.)
G. S. Chapus. France: Librairie A. S. Sahy, 1930. 308p.
The author was a teacher at a secondary school in Antananarivo, and a member of the Académie malgache. The first part of the book analyses the development of the system of education before 1895. This is followed by a comparison between Madagascar and other French colonies with an evaluation of the level of education during the reign of the King Radama I and the effects of the rivalries between the different religious groups in the field of education. The second part is about the organization of education in 1895 according to region, showing how the central plateau was clearly favoured. A chapter deals with the role of the London Missionary Society in education.

271 **L'enfant et son éducation dans la civilisation traditionnelle malgache.**
(The child and his education in the traditional Malagasy civilization.)
Pierre Randrianarisoa. Fandriana, Madagascar: the Author, 1981.
144p. bibliog.
This important sociological study looks at the education of children from infancy to adulthood in the context of their traditional and cultural background. The author studies the cultural aspects of Madagascar in some detail, including the 'ways of the ancestors'.

272 **Keep the goal in mind.**
Justine Ranivosoa. *Teachers of the World*, no. 3 (1986), p. 23-26.
This magazine was published in the former German Democratic Republic. Written in strongly socialist language, the article outlines the problems facing teachers in Malagasy schools in the mid 1980s: malnutrition, banditry, and the necessity to take other jobs to augment the teachers' pay. The subject is approached from the woman's point of view in 'Power to the people's elbow: women teachers in Madagascar' by J. Martin. *Teachers of the World*, no. 3 (1989), p. 25-26. But this is a very general piece with few examples specific to Madagascar.

Education

Africa South of the Sahara.
See item no. 7.

Literature and Poetry

Traditional poetry and literature

273 **Contes de Madagascar.** (Tales of Madagascar.)
   Collected by Zefaniasy Bemananjara.   Paris: Conseil International de
   la Langue Française, 1980. 146p.
Twenty-four short traditional stories in French.

274 **Hainteny: the traditional poetry of Madagascar.**
   Translated, with an introduction and notes by Leonard Fox.   London;
   Toronto: Associated University Presses, 1990. 464p.
Here are 457 *hainteny* poems with the Malagasy text facing the English translation.
The book is divided into two major sections: 'Love' and 'Life', then further subdivided
into subjects such as good and evil, wisdom and foolishness, poverty and wealth, pride,
mockery and humour, parents and children, war and death. The poems are beautifully
translated, readily accessible to English readers and powerfully evocative of their
Malagasy themes. Further understanding of the Merina culture which created *hainteny*
is provided in the author's excellent introduction.

275 **Contes de côte ouest de Madagascar.** (Tales of the western coastal area
   of Madagascar.)
   N. J. Gueunier.   Paris; Antananarivo: Karthala Ambozontany, 1985.
   197p.
Twelve traditional stories collected and translated by Gueunier between 1977 and
1984, in Malagasy and French.

276 **Malagasy tale index.**
Lee Haring. Helsinki: Suomalainen Tiedeakakatemia Academia
Scientiarum Fennica, 505p. bibliog. (FF Communications Series
no. 231).
An inventory of some 850 narratives collected and published in French or English
translations between 1655 and 1976.

277 **Verbal arts in Madagascar: performance in historical perspective.**
Lee Haring. Philadelphia: University of Pennsylvania Press, 1992.
242p. (Publications of the American Folklore Society).
This important work combines a history of the encounter between Europeans and
colonized people with an analysis of four types of Malagasy folklore: riddles; proverbs;
'hainteny'; and oratory. The author contends that Europeans trivialized Malagasy
reality by creating a vision of folklore. He reconstructs the performance of the texts in
their social contexts.

20th-century poetry

278 **Jean-Joseph Rabearivelo et la mort.** (Jean-Joseph Rabearivelo and
death.)
Robert Boudry. Paris: Presence Africaine, 1958. 84p.
Jean-Joseph Rabearivelo is considered Madagascar's foremost poet, and a precursor of
'négritude'. Born in 1901, he committed suicide in 1937. This is probably the best
appraisal of his life and work.

279 **Voices of negritude.**
Julio Finn. New York; London: Quartet Books, 1988. 246p. bibliog.
This book contains some excellent biographical material on the Malagasy poets
Rabearivelo and Rabemananjara.

280 **Rabearivelo: 24 poems.**
Jean-Joseph Rabearivelo, translated by Ulli Beier, Gerard Moore.
Ibadan, Nigeria: Mbari, 1962. 20p.
An English translation of Madagascar's best-known poet, nicely designed and
illustrated with black-and-white drawings.

281 **Translations from the night: selected poems.**
Jean-Joseph Rabearivelo, translated by John Reed and Clive Wake.
London; Nairobi; Lusaka; Ibadan: Heinemann Educational, 1975. 73p.
(African Writers Series).
Jean-Joseph Rabearivelo wrote in both Malagasy and French (and also Spanish), his
mature poems fusing the French free style with traditional Malagasy *hainteny*. This
volume of his poems has English and French versions on opposite pages.

282 **Anthologie de la poésie nègre et malgache.** (Anthology of negro and
Malagasy poetry.)
Leopold Sédar Senghor. Presses Universitaires de France, 1948. 227p.

A collection of Malagasy poems, written in French, with biographies of the poets:
Jean-Joseph Rabearivelo, Jacques Rabemananjara and Flavien Ranaivo.

283 **Black and blue: the life and lyrics of Andy Razaf.**
Barry Singer. New York: Schirmer Books, 1992. 444p. bibliog.

Andy Razaf is famous for his collaboration with Fats Waller on songs such as 'Ain't
misbehavin' ' and 'Black and blue' and other classics of the 1920s and 1930s. His name
is an anglicized and shortened version of Andriamantena Paul Razafinkeriefo; he was
the grand-nephew of Queen Ranavalona III, the last monarch of Madagascar. Razaf's
mother was the daughter of John Waller, one of the first black American diplomats,
being US consul in Madagascar in the 1890s; see *Black odyssey: John L. Waller and the
promise of American life* (q.v.). Although this book is largely about Razaf's music and
life in New York, it throws interesting light on his Malagasy ancestry.

284 **J.-J. Rabearivelo, a poet before nègritude.**
Clive Wake. In *The critical evaluation of African literature.* Edited by
Edgar Wright. London: Heinemann, 1973. p. 149-72.

This paper presents an evaluation of Rabearivelo's life and work. In the comparative
isolation of Madagascar he published a number of volumes of poetry before the
négritude poetical movement was fully developed. Writing in French, his poetry is, like
that of his successors, a product of the colonial situation. In his later poems he
incorporated the techniques and themes of the traditional Malagasy *hainteny* poetry.
There are extracts from his poems throughout the chapter.

Novels

285 **Sa majesté Ranavalona III, ma reine.** (Her majesty Ranavalona III,
my queen.)
D. Boyer. Paris: Fasquelle, 1946. 255p.

An almost biographical novel with a strong historical background. The story starts with
the crowning of Queen Ranavalona III, continuing with the role of her prime minister
in her downfall, her subsequent exile in Algeria and her death.

286 **The rig.**
John Collee. London: Viking, 1991. 373p.

Modern novels set in Madagascar are rare. John Collee has researched the background
very carefully, and all the Madagascar details in this fast-moving thriller are accurate.
The rig is the last from a supposedly fruitless five-year search for oil. As the last team
leaves their plane explodes in mid-air. Were they murdered to conceal information of
an oil find?

Literature and Poetry. Novels

287 **Ranavalo, reine cruelle.** (Ranavalo, the cruel queen.)
Pierre Sogno. France: Roman-Ramsay, 1990. 369p.

A novel loosely based on the life and reign of the Queen Ranavalona I (1828-1861). Mavo wanted to be a queen, her aim was the throne and her means the power of feminine charm. Once crowned, her life was based on pleasure and fanaticism. This novel is well researched and written in a lively style to produce a convincing and entertaining story.

288 **The deadly lady of Madagascar.**
C. V. Terry. London; Melbourne; New York: Jarrolds, 1959. 238p.

A rollicking novel centred on the adventures of Richard Douglas, first mate in the service of the East India Company, who is sent on a secret mission to Madagascar in the early part of the 18th century. The 'deadly lady' is the daughter of a Portuguese merchant. The historical information should not be taken too seriously.

289 **King Radama's word: John Aikins's adventures in Madagascar.**
Robert Thynne. London: John Hogg, 1899. 244p.

A novel based on actual people and events, taking one of the more bloodthirsty periods of Madagascar's history as its theme. It is hard to read since much of the dialogue is in dialect.

290 **At spear point.**
C. M. Whitfield. London: Edinburgh House, 1953. 119p.

This is an adventure story for children, but written with knowledge and affection by a resident of Madagascar, and concerning the 1947 uprising.

Princes et paysans: Les Tañala de l'Ikongo. (Princes and peasants: the Tañala of the Ikongo).
See item no. 162.

Arts and Crafts

General

291 Notes on the Madagascar collection.
Philadelphia: Philadelphia Museum, 1906.
A nicely-illustrated catalogue with clear text and black-and-white photographs of the artefacts in the museum, such as lambas, hats, pottery and musical instruments.

292 L'art malgache. (Malagasy arts.)
Marcelle Urbain-Flaublée.   Paris: Presse Universitaire de France, 1963. 128p. bibliog. (Pays d'Outre-Mer, vol 5, no. 2).
This is a study of the evolution of Malagasy traditional arts: funeral monuments; circumcision poles; and sacred houses. Also examined are the religious arts of amulets and other 'magic' decorative arts. Originally the author studied the Oceanic and Indonesian arts, and this led him to have closer look at Madagascar.

Music

293 Stern's guide to contemporary African music.
Ronnie Graham.   London: Pluto, 1989. 352p.
This book covers all the major musical styles in Africa, including Madagascar, with biographies of the leading musicians and a discography of their major recordings.

294 **Musical instruments and history in Madagascar.**
N. McLeod. In: *Essays for a humanist, an offering to Klaus Wachsmann.* New York: Town House Press, 1977. p. 189-215.

This book is a privately-printed collection of essays presented to Klaus Wachsmann, an ethnomusicologist and Professor of Music at UCLA, on his seventieth birthday. In this essay the author looks at theories on the origins of the Malagasy people as revealed by their music and musical instruments. She examines all the instruments and draws tentative conclusions as to their place of origin – Indonesia or Africa.

295 **Les instruments de musique de Madagascar.** (Musical instruments of Madagascar.)
Curt Sachs. Paris: Institut d'Ethnologie, 1938. 96p. plus 15p. photographs. (Travaux et Mémoires de l'Institut d'Ethnologie, 28).

A scholarly work which clearly portrays the different musical instruments of Madagascar, illustrated with black-and-white drawings and photographs. The author describes how the instruments are made and gives regional Malagasy names. This is the definitive book on the subject.

Textiles and weaving

296 **Malagasy textiles.**
John Mack. Aylesbury, England: Shire, 1989. 60p.

Cloth, to the Malagasy, is an essential part of both life and death. In this survey of the rich variety of textiles in Madagascar, the author, director of the Museum of Mankind in London, discusses the range of materials used and techniques involved, and examines the highly elaborate patterning and their significance. The book concludes with a useful list of museums in the UK, USA, France and Madagascar with collections of Malagasy textiles.

297 **Lamba Malagasy: étoffes traditionelles malgaches. Exposition organisée par le Musée d'Art et Archéologie de l'Université.**
(Malagasy 'lamba': traditional Malagasy fabrics. An exhibition organized by the University Museum of Art and Archaeology.)
Arranged by Chantal Radimilahy. Antananarivo: Université de Madagascar, 1978. 50p.

The lamba, a rectangle of cotton or silk material, could be considered as the national dress of Madagascar. Colours, designs, and ways of wearing them vary according to region and ethnic group. This is a catalogue with black-and-white illustrations showing the different lambas, their history, weaving techniques and the meaning revealed in different ways of wearing them.

298 **Étude sur la fabrication des lambamena.** (Study on the weaving of the
lambamena.)
E. Vernier. *Journal de la Societé des Africanistes*, vol. 34, no. 1
(1964), p. 7-34.

This article begins with a history of silk-weaving in Madagascar, from the introduction
of the silkworm and its food source the mulberry tree by the British in 1826. It then
goes on to describe the technique of spinning, dyeing, and weaving the *lambamena*, or
burial shroud.

Cuisine

299 **Cuisine malgache, cuisine Creole.** (Malagasy cooking, creole cooking.)
Pierre Boissard. Antananarivo: Librairie de Madagascar, 1976. 144p.
This is written in both French and Malagasy. There are some background stories but basically this is a recipe book aimed at the French expatriate. Notes describe unusual ingredients, and there is a French/Malagasy dictionary of food.

300 **Vanilla cookbook.**
Patricia Rain. Berkeley, California: Celestial Arts, 1983. 124p.
The book begins with a history of vanilla cultivation and the process of turning an exotic orchid (introduced from Mexico) into one of Madagascar's main exports. The main section contains recipes for cooking both sweet and savoury dishes with vanilla.

Recreation

301 **Fanorona: the national game of Madagascar.**
Leonard Fox.   Charleston, Carolina: International Fanorona
Association, 1984. 44p.

Fanorona is a board game of tactical skill, roughly comparable with chess or draughts, but unique. As well as having a popular international following, the game has played a major role in the history and culture of the Malagasy people. The book contains a history of the game, detailed rules and instructions, tactics and illustrative games.

Philately and Numismatics

Philately

302 **Timbres de Madagascar: de 1859 au 1er Janvier 1972.** (Stamps of
Madagascar: from 1859 to January 1 1972.)
M. Marcel Brambilla.   Antananarivo: L'Administration des Postes et
Télécommunications, 1972. 324p.

Nearly one thousand examples of stamps are shown. Early chapters deal with the
Merina period (from 1859) through the French conquest (1894-1896) to the French
colonial period up to 1958. The modern period of post-independence takes up a further
one hundred pages. A useful bibliography completes this exhaustive work.

Numismatics

303 **Les premières monnaies de Madagascar.** (The first coins of
Madagascar.)
J. Chauvicourt, S. Chauvicourt.   *Bulletin de Madagascar*, no. 261
(Feb. 1968), 27p. bibliog.

In its early days of contact with the West, Madagascar's coinage comprised silver coins
from European countries cut into pieces. Travellers had to carry a pair of scales with
them, and when making a purchase a specified quantity of these fragments was
weighed in the presence of the vendor. This 'cut money' is of great interest to
collectors.

304 **Numismatique malgache.** (Malagasy numismatics.)
Tananarive: Industrie Graphique, 1965-69. 5 vols.

The subjects of the five volumes are: vol. 1. 'Les monnaies frappées pour Madagascar, 1667-1965' (Coins minted for Madagascar, 1667-1965); vol. 2. 'Les monnaies Françaises et de l'union latine à Madagascar' (French coins and those of the 'Latin union' of Madagascar), i.e. the associated islands of the Indian Ocean; vol. 3. 'Les premières monnaies introduites à Madagascar' (The first coins introduced into Madagascar); vol. 4. 'La monnaie coupée et les poids monétaires de Madagascar' (Cut money and the monetary weights of Madagascar); and vol. 5. 'Médailles et décorations de Madagascar' (Medals and decorations of Madagascar).

305 **The cut money of Madagascar.**
F. Pridmore. Extract from *The Numismatic Circular and Catalogue for Sale by Spink & Son*, vol. 61, no. 11 (Nov. 1953).

This extract forms the basis for the article by J. & S. Chauvicourt in *Bulletin de Madagascar* (q.v.).

Africa South of the Sahara.
See item no. 7.

Newspapers and Periodicals

Daily newspapers

306 **Bulletin de l'Agence Nationale d'Information 'Tanatra' (ANTA).**
(Bulletin of the National Information Agency [ANTA].)
Antananarivo, 1977- . daily.

A government information bulletin in French. During the Ratsiraka regime this was the only source of foreign news, although it was heavily edited and censored.

307 **Madagascar Tribune.**
Antananarivo: Rahaga Ramaholimihaso, 1988- . daily.

A tabloid, pro-government newspaper in French, aimed at a more educated readership than *Midi Madagasikara* (q.v.) with a circulation of 12,000.

308 **Midi Madagasikara.** (Madagascar Midday.)
Antananarivo: Zo Rakotoseheno, 1983- . daily.

A tabloid newspaper in French and Malagasy with a circulation of 20,005. Its emphasis is on sensationalism, with the minimum of news content. It is said to be the best for small advertisements and for 'Births and Deaths'!

309 **Nouveau Journal de Madagascar.** (New Newspaper of Madagascar.)
Antananarivo: Johary Rakotonirina, 1993- . daily.

The previous names of this newspaper were *Madagascar Matin* and *Journal de Madagascar*. It tends to change its name with changes in government and to follow the government line in propaganda. In French and Malagasy, with occasional articles in English. Circulation 8,000.

Weekly publications

310   **DMD (Dans les Média Domain).** (In the Media Tomorrow.)
Antananarivo: Nouvelle Société de Presse et d'Editions, 1986- .
weekly.
An independent publication in French aimed at an educated, middle-class readership.
It has a circulation of 2,650.

311   **Fanavaozana/Le Renouveau.** (Renewal.)
Antananarivo: Ammi Rasoanindrainy, 1989- . weekly.
The publication of the political party, AKFM Renouveau, this journal has a circulation
of 5,000.

312   **Iloafo.** (Leader.)
Antananarivo, 1990-1993. weekly.
The publication of the Iloafo Society, a group of politically active members from the
liberal professions, such as university lecturers and business people.

313   **Journal Officiel de la République de Madagascar.** (Official Newspaper
of the Republic of Madagascar.)
Antananarivo: Imprimerie Nationale, 1883- . weekly.
This contains government information in French and Malagasy, concerning laws,
decrees and ordinances, official notices, legal notices, etc. This is essential reading for
businesses in Madagascar, and has a circulation of 6,200.

314   **PME Madagascar.**
Antananarivo: Charles Ranarijesy, 1988- . weekly.
The title means: 'Petites et Moyennes Entreprises/Petites et Moyennes Industries'. It
offers advice in French to small businesses and entrepeneurs, and has a circulation of
1,000.

Monthly publications

315   **Confidences au Sommet.** (Confidences at the Top.)
Antananarivo. monthly.
This is not an under-cover publication! It offers analysis and opinion on government
policies.

316   **Gazety Medikaly.** (Medical gazette.)
Antananarivo. 1965- . monthly.
This contains medical information. It has a circulation of 2,000.

317 **Journal Scientifique de Madagascar.** (Scientific Journal of Madagascar.)
Antananarivo. 1985- . monthly.
This has a circulation of 3,000.

318 **JURECO.**
Antananarivo: JURECO S.A., 1986- . monthly.
A serious publication, in French, on business, law and economics, edited by experts. It
has a circulation of 2,200.

319 **Revue de l'Océan Indien.**
Antananarivo: Communications et Medias de l'Ocean Indien, 1981- .
monthly.
This gives regional news and information in French. It has a circulation of 2,000.

Quarterly publications

320 **Brief.**
Antananarivo: Cabinets Ramoaholimaso Mana-Mihaso, 1985- .
quarterly.
This is a technical publication for businesses, with a circulation of 500, produced by a
firm of auditors and accountants.

321 **Carrefour des Sciences.** (Crossroads of the Sciences.)
Antananarivo: Ministère de Recherche Scientifique, 1992- . quarterly.
Published by university students to encourage student research, to provide information
on university life and the professions, to offer advice with the help of university
professors, and to encourage team work. The circulation is 600.

322 **Hanitriniala.**
Antananarivo: Association Nationale pour la Gestion des Aires
Protégées, 1993- . quarterly.
This publication covers environmental matters and ecotourism. The name is Malagasy
for 'Scent of the forest'.

323 **Matoy.**
Antananarivo: Ministère d'Etat à d'Agriculture, 1990- . quarterly.
This is a journal of agricultural news with a circulation of 1,000. 'Matoy' means
'maturity'.

Others

324   MADA Economie.
Antananarivo: Richard Claude Rakotonaivo, 1977- . irregular.
Reports on economic affairs in south-east Africa. It has a circulation of 5,000, and appears monthly at irregular intervals.

325   Recherche et Culture. (Research and Culture.)
Antananarivo: University of Antananarivo, 1985- . biannual.
Published by the French department of the University, this has a circulation of 1,000.

326   Vaovao FJKM. (FJKM News.)
Antananarivo: FJKM, ten times a year.
The journal of Fiangonan'i Jesoa Kristy eto Madagascar (the Church of Jesus Christ in Madagascar). This is a Protestant church organization. Their publication appears ten times a year in Malagasy and five times a year in French and English.

Archive newspapers and journals

327   Antananarivo Annual and Madagascar Magazine.
Edited by J. Sibree, R. Baron.   Antananarivo: London Missionary Society Press, 1877-1900.
The Annual, founded by two of the great names in the London Missionary Society, stated its aims as: 'A record of information on the topography and natural productions of Madagascar and the customs, traditions, language, and religious beliefs of its people'. The Hardyman Collection (SOAS) has the volumes from the early 1880s to 1892. There is much valuable information here.

328   Bulletin de l'Académie malgache. (Bulletin of the Malagasy Academy.)
Tananarive: Imprimerie malgache, 1902- . annual.
The Académie malgache was founded in 1902 by The French Governor-General of Madagascar, Joseph Gallieni. Modelled on the Académie Française, it concerns itself with a whole range of scholarship about Madagascar, including all the sciences. The Bulletin reflects this range in its publication of papers presented to the Academy. Volumes dating from 1902 may be viewed in the Hardyman Collection (SOAS). Occasional issues have appeared in recent years.

329   Madagascar News.
Antananarivo: E. Underwood Harvey, 1890-9-? weekly.
The newspaper was published entirely in English and had as its motto: 'Madagascar for the Malagasy and her commerce for all countries'. It replaced *The Madagascar Times* (q.v.) and had a similar editorial policy. It probably ceased publication before the French takeover in 1895. The Hardyman Collection (SOAS) has copies from 1890-91.

Newspapers and Periodicals. Archive newspapers and journals

330 **Madagascar Times.**
Antananarivo: Anthony Tacchi, 1882-90. weekly.
This newspaper appeared during the decade when the French were tightening their grip on Madagascar, and was outspoken in its defence of Madagascar's sovereignty against French encroachments. It contained local political and social news, political comment, commercial information, and advertisements for various products. It is trilingual: French, Malagasy, and English in three columns. Bound copies from 1882-86 and 1889-90 may be viewed in the Hardyman Collection (SOAS).

331 **La Revue de Madagascar.** (The Madagascar Review.)
Tananarive: Imprimerie Officielle, 1933-1941?; 1949-1972. three times per year.
The Review was issued under the auspices of the Bureau des Informations of the French colonial government, and covered all aspects of Malagasy life: social, economic, intellectual and cultural. After a break during the war and the post-war years, it resumed publication in 1949 and continued until 1972 when Madagascar broke its links with France. The Hardyman Collection (SOAS) has a complete collection. Each issue was well-printed and illustrated with woodcuts.

Africa South of the Sahara.
See item no. 7.

Bibliographies

General

332 **Bibliographie Annuelle de Madagascar.** (Annual Bibliography of
Madagascar.)
Antananarivo: Bibliotheque Universitaire et Bibliotheque Nationale,
1964- . annual.
This national bibliography is organized into sections according to subject and cross-
referenced by author. It is not annotated.

333 **Madagascar: a selected list of references.**
Helen F. Conover, under the direction of Florence S. Hellman.
Washington, DC: Library of Congress, 1942. 22p.
This is a reproduced typescript, so it is not easy to read. Nevertheless, it is useful for
reference purposes.

334 **Madagascar (the Malagasy Republic): a list of materials in the African
collections of Stanford University and the Hoover Institution on War,
Revolution and Peace.**
Peter Duignan.   Stanford, California: Stanford University and Hoover
Institution, 1962. 25p.
Although there is no annotation, this is a very useful bibliography of Madagascar up to
the early 1960s. It contains an incomplete list of confidential microfilmed British
documents and government documents published in Antananarivo.

335 **Bibliographie de Madagascar.** (Bibliography of Madagascar.)
Guillerme Grandidier.   Paris: Comité de Madagascar, 1906. 905p.
The entries are arranged alphabetically by author. There is a large 'anonymous' section
and the work also includes periodicals. In 1933 Grandidier published another volume

covering works published since 1905, and in 1955 a further volume covering 1934-55 was produced. This was followed by the *Bibliographie nationale de Madagascar: 1956-1963* edited by Jean Fontvielle (Antananarivo: Université de Madagascar, 1971). From 1964 onwards the *Bibliographie Annuelle de Madagascar* (q.v.) has been published.

336 **South-East Central Africa and Madagascar: general, ethnology/ sociology, linguistics.**
Ruth Jones. London: International African Institute, 1961. 53p. (Africa Bibliography Series).
This bibliography is based on the bibliographical card index of the International African Institute. The Madagascar section is on p.38-47, and is also available as a separate extract. The majority of the entries are in French.

337 **A guide to manuscripts and documents in the British Isles relating to Africa.**
Compiled by Noel Matthews, M. Doreen Wainwright, edited by J. D. Pearson. London: Oxford University Press, 1971. 321p.
The list includes eighty entries for Madagascar to be found in some twenty libraries and archives in Britain.

338 **Périodique malgaches de la Bibliothèque Nationale.** (Malagasy periodicals in the National Library.)
Germaine Razafintsalama, Rasoahanta Randrianarivelo. Paris: Bibliothèque Nationale, 1970.
This is a well-produced, clearly laid out bibliography. Entries are in alphabetical order.

339 **Madagascar and adjacent islands: a guide to official publications.**
Julian W. Witherell. Washington, DC: Library of Congress, 1965. 58p.
The entries are not annotated and the mimeographed pages are difficult to read.

Natural history

340 **Coral reefs and coastal zone of Toliara: bibliography.**
Andrew Cooke. Antananarivo: World Wide Fund for Nature, 1992. 29p.
This is a typewritten list, available from the WWF (B.P. 738, Antananarivo 101) compiled as part of an ecotourism project in Madagascar's south-west region. It contains 381 items covering a wide range of specialized academic subjects. There is a good selection of entries for mangroves and their ecology. About half the entries are in French.

341 **Madagascan orchids: an annotated bibliography.**
Johan Hermans, Clare Hermans.   Enfield, England: the Authors,
1992. 31p.

This exhaustive bibliography, compiled by orchid enthusiasts and available from the
authors (17 Rosewood Drive, Crews Hill, Enfield, Middlesex, EN2 9BT), lists and
describes most available references, including a large number of descriptions of new
species. It is updated annually. Entries are mainly drawn from the British *Orchid
Review* and the American *Orchid Society Bulletin*.

Indexes

There follow three separate indexes: authors (personal and corporate), editors and translators; titles; and subjects. Title entries are italicized and refer either to the main titles, or to other works cited in the annotations. The numbers refer to bibliographic entry rather than page numbers. Individual index entries are arranged in alphabetical sequence.

Index of Authors

Index of Titles

Index of Subjects

116

Map of Madagascar

This map shows the more important towns and other features.

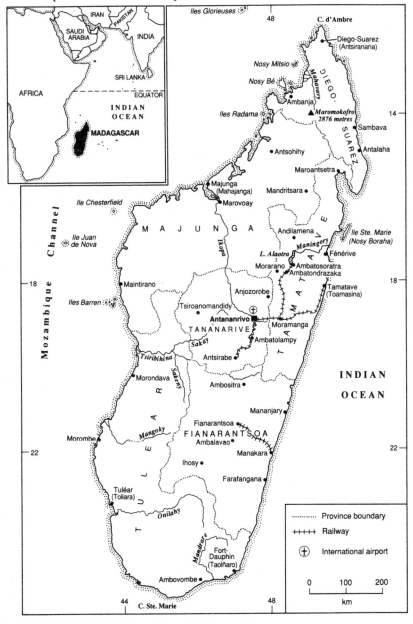